Gregor Janknecht
and the Franciscans
in Nineteenth Century
United States and Europe

Essays by Kirsten Rakemann Schmies

and Stephan Scherfenberg

Translated from German by Stephan Scherfenberg

Library of Congress Cataloging-in-Publication Data

Gregor Janknecht and the Franciscans in nineteenth century United States and Europe / essays by Kirsten Rakemann Schmies and Stephan Scherfenberg; translated from German by Stephan Scherfenberg.
   p. cm.
  ISBN 0-88382-263-6 (alk. paper)
  1. Janknecht, Gregor, 1829-1896. 2. Franciscans—Europe—History. 3. Franciscans—United States—History. I. Schmies, Kirsten Rakemann. II. Scherfenberg, Stephan.

  BX4705.J36G7413 2008
  271'.302--dc22
  [B]

                            2008013332

Academy of American Franciscan History
Berkeley, California

Editor's Note

The present volume consists of essays written by two German scholars and translated into English by Stephan Scherfenberg. Stephan received his Masters in North American Studies at the Free University of Berlin. Kirsten Rakemann Schmies was a resident scholar at the Institute for Franciscan History in Muenster, Germany for ten years. She currently teaches History and Religion at Hittorf-High School in Recklinghausen, Germany. Her husband, Bernard Schmies, is Director of the Institute for Franciscan Research in Muenster. Though we translated the essays into English we have left the footnotes and some phrases in the Germanic style.

This is one of the Academy's first efforts at publishing materials on Franciscans in the United States, outside of mission and borderland studies. We hope that this will inspire future work on Franciscans in the nineteenth and twentieth centuries in the United States and Canada.

Special thanks to Brother David Buer, OFM, for facilitating this project. Without his determination it would never have come to fruition. Thanks to Mrs. Denise Thuston, archivist for the Sacred Heart Province, and to the Franciscans of Sacred Heart for their generous support.

Contents

Very Rev. Fr. Gregory Janknecht, Founder of Sacred Heart Provence

Gregory Janknecht,
Five Time Franciscan Provincial,
1855-1891

BY KIRSTEN RAKEMANN SCHMIES

"In my opinion it is impossible to give an adequate picture of the personality of Pater Gregory with all its bright and dark sides. The official Gregory can be portrayed according to the files. The rest is based on the memories of brothers who were young at his time and could not have known P. Gregory very well. They were under a great man's spell and could not look behind the scenes. If we had reports from men such as Othmar Maasmann, Ambrosius Dreimüller, Irenäus Bierbaum and others, we would get a much more adequate picture. Even with full respect for his huge accomplishments, the person of P. Gregory still has to be judged with caution."[1]

So wrote P. Willibald Kullmann to P. Manfred Loddenkötter on March 10, 1930. At that time both men were writing biographies of Gregory Janknecht which are the most comprehensive accounts to date.[2] Besides that there is an overwhelming number of short biographies about this Provincial, who shaped the developments of the Sacred Heart Province in the second half of the 19th century as no one else had done. Despite the large amount of literature, almost the whole biographic historiography about Janknecht comes from within the Order. There has been little new research since 1930.[3]

---

[1] ASFP Werl, Personal File of P. Gregory Janknecht; letter from P. Willibald Kullmann to P. Manfred Loddenkötter, Düsseldorf March 10, 1930.

[2] Kullmann, Willibald: "P Gregor Janknecht" In: *Vita Seraphica* 10 (1929) 52-58, 99-108; Loddenkötter, Manfred: "P Gregor Janknechts Verdienste um die sächsische Provinz vom Hl. Kreuze" In: *Franziskanische Studien* 17 (1930) 211-227.

[3] Two of the newer biographies but with few new perspectives are Griesenbrock, Heribert: "P. Gregor Janknecht" In: *Neubegründer der Franziskanermission in Brasilien.* Edited by the Missionsverwaltung der Franziskaner. (Werl, 1992) 4-21 and Büning, Heinz: "Pater Gregor Janknecht." In: Büning, Hans (Editor): *Kirchhellener, die man lernen sollte.* (Kirchhellen, 1983) 320-335.

Consequently, the continuing research on the Saxonian Province as well as new sources[4] provide a new look at the person of P. Gregory Janknecht after more than 70 years.

1. The Years Before His Election as Provincial in 1855[5]

After the restoration of the Saxonian Franciscan province in 1627, Westfalia became the main source of origin for most members of the province. This was also true for Gregory Janknecht. Born September 29, 1829, on a farm belonging to Kirchhellen, he was named Theodor Overgünne, but he was called Dierk Janknecht. The next day his parents, the farmer Johann Heinrich Overgünne and Angela née Langweg, baptized him in the old village church of St. John.[6] The name Janknecht comes from the farm's name which belonged to his grandmother, Anna Cath. Overgünne née Janknecht.[7]

Dierk was the oldest of five siblings. The second son, Johann Theodor, was born on July 19, 1831. Later he took over the farm. The third brother, Werner, was born on August 26,1833, and also became a farmer. He was followed by a sister Elisabeth, born on

---

[4] Janknecht's very extensive correspondence has to be mentioned. Parts of his letters were published in the 1940s and 1950s by Julius Reinhold. However, they were hardly considered by the later biographers. There are also letters to the General. See Reinhold, Julius: "Aus der römischen Korrespondenz des P. Gregor Janknecht über die Jahre 1871-1879. [Kulturkampf, Exil, Errichtung der Tochterprovinz vom Heiligsten Herzen Jesu in Nordamerika]" In: *Vita Seraphica* 29 (1948) 47-82 there are letters to Bernhard Döbbing, who later became Bishop of Nepi-Sutri in Italy. There are more than 100 letters which Janknecht wrote between 1883 and 1886. So far, these letters have only been analyzed with regard to the mission in Brazil. However, they are a source for many other aspects of the History of the Saxonian Province. See Reinhold, Julius:"Übersicht über den neu aufgefundenen persönlichen Nachlaß Bischofs Bernhard Döbbing" In: *Vita Seraphica* 36 (1955) 232-240, especially 238. Today, these letters are in the Provincial Archives in Werl.

[5] The following dates are mostly from Loddenkötter, "P. Gregor" and Kullmann, "P. Gregor." Some of them are from Janknecht's neighbors in Kirchhellen or memories of older friars.

[6] The church was destroyed by a fire in 1917 and soon replaced by a new building. See: Büning, Hans: *1000 Jahre St. Johannes Kirchhellen.*(Kirchhellen, 1985) 47.

[7] Even at school P. Gregory Janknecht was enrolled under the farm's name. See Loddenkötter, „P. Gregor „211 as well as the list of pupils in Schwarz, Wilhelm: *Festschrift zur Einweihung des neuen Gymnasialgebäudes und zur Feier des 260jähri. Jubiläums der höheren Lehranstalt in Dorsten.* (Dorsten, 1902) 36.

August 7, 1836.[8] The youngest sister, Anna Maria, born January 12, 1840, died at the age of three on March 21, 1843.[9]

Janknecht spent his childhood on his parent's farm. He probably attended the village school like most of the children.[10] Soon, the young Janknecht received private lessons from the pastor of Kirchhellen, Wilhelm Feldmann.[11] This oldest son had special talents so that his parents decided to allow him to continue on for higher education. Since advanced education was not necessary for running a farm, it is likely that he was already destined for the priesthood. This would explain the private lessons which were a prerequisite to pass the entrance examinations into the college at Dorsten.[12] Interestingly, no other member of the Janknecht and Overgünne families had ever attended this college in the 19th century.[13]

At the age of 12 Janknecht entered the college, which also meant he had to move from Kirchellen to Dorsten, since the distance would have been too far to walk every day. This was not unusual because there were only very few schools of higher education at this time. Many other students came from places even farther away than Kirchhellen.[14] Unfortunately, it cannot be determined where Dierk lived during his time in Dorsten.

It was probably during his time at college that Janknecht first came into contact with the Franciscan Order. The college in Dorsten had been founded by Franciscans in 1642. Members of the Order taught

---

[8] Elisabeth also chose the Franciscan life. On October 30, 1858 she entered the "Third Order" as a nurse in St. Mauritz (Münster). She started the novitiate on June 2, 1860 and made her profession as Sister Ignatia on August 24, 1861. She died of tuberculosis on November 17, 1888 in the house in Hasselünne, which she had led for several years as Guardian.

[9] See Personal file P. Gregory Janknecht, letter Fr. Dietrich Frerick to P. Willibald Kullmann (Dorsten, March 24, 1929) according to the registry in Kirchhellen.

[10] Büning, Pater Gregor 320.

[11] Büning, *1000 Jahre* 184-186.

[12] The rules of the college in 1820 said: "Every pupil, who wishes to be enrolled, has to demonstrate his abilities in a special exam. German and Latin have to be complete in reading and writing. He needs to know the 4 species. . . ." Kork, Maximilian Joseph: „Beiträge zur Geschichte des Progymnasiums zu Dorsten 1867", 3-14, Tl. 2, in: *Jahresbericht des vollberechtigten katholischen Progymnasiums zu Dorsten 1868*, 1-15; here 3.

[13] Schwarz, *Festschrift* 3-87.

[14] Ibid. 102-118.

there until 1823; in fact there were Franciscans among the faculty until 1837.[15] By Janknecht's time the Friars were not directly involved in the school anymore. Because of the Secularization the number of Friars decreased significantly and the Franciscans were no longer capable of running the college.[16] Nevertheless the relationship with the friary remained, since the school was very close to the convent. Furthermore, the Franciscans still celebrated Mass for the students at the school. The Guardian of the friary probably had a beneficial influence on the relationship between the school and the college. Ferdinand Volbach, Guardian of the friary in Dorsten from 1837-1846, had taught at the college from 1817 until 1833.[17] Thus, he had a personal interest in the relationship between both institutions. This became very clear on the occasion of the college's bicentennial anniversary in 1842. The Guardian was invited as guest of honor and brought the school a newly consecrated flag. In addition, the Franciscan friary played an important role in the celebration.[18] This was Janknecht's second year at the college and also the year of his confirmation.[19]

After four years, Janknecht had to transfer to the grammar school in Recklinghausen in 1845 in order to pass the Abitur. This school also had Franciscan roots. From its foundation in 1730 until 1825 it

---

[15] See Schmies, Bernd / Rakemann, Kirsten: *Spuren franziskanischer Geschichte. Chronologischer Abriß der Geschichte der Sächsischen Franziskanerprovinz von ihren Anfängen bis zur Gegenwart.* Ed. Dieter Berg. (Werl 1999) (Saxonia Franciscana, Special Edition) 361 and 467. For literature about the Dorsten college see Kordwittenborg, Hans-Ulrich / Nickel, Ralf: *Bibliographie zur Geschichte der Sächsischen Franziskanerprovinz. Bd. 1: Franziskaner in Westfalen.* Ed. Dieter Berg. (Werl,) 1994 (Saxonia Franciscana, 4) 339-348. Also Kistenich, Johannes: *Bettelmönche im öffentlichen Schulwesen. Ein Handbuch der Erzdiözese Köln 1600 bis 1850.* (Köln-Weimar-Wien, 2001), 576-657.

[16] Kistenich, *Bettelmönche* 586. The situation did not improve during the following years. See also: Schwarz, Wilhelm: Nachträge zu der „Festschrift zur Einweihung des neuen Gymnasialgebäudes und zur Feier des 260jährigen Jubiläums der höheren Lehranstalt in Dorsten." In: Schwarz, Wilhelm: *Katholisches Progymnasium (in Entw. zum Gymnasium) mit Ersatzunterricht für das Griechische zu Dorsten. Bericht über das Schuljahr 1902.* (Dorsten, 1903), 21-30.

[17] Griesenbrock, Heribert: *500 Jahre Franziskaner in Dorsten 1488-1988.* (Werl, 1988), 162.

[18] Buerbaum, Joseph: *Beschreibung der zweiten Sekular-Feier des Progymnasiums zu Dorsten.* (Münster, 1843), especially 3-5, 48, 63.

[19] AG OFM Rom, C40 (Historia Provinciae S. Crucis) fol. 149v.

was under Franciscan leadership.[20] However, the Recklinghausen friary was closed in 1835 so that the Order was no longer present there. Janknecht probably chose this school because of its proximity to Kirchhellen and Dorsten.[21] Two other students also transferred with Janknecht from Dorsten to Recklinghausen.[22] Janknecht probably lived in Recklinghausen and not on his parents' farm in Kirchhellen. However there are no sources to confirm that.

He finished the Abitur with the exams on August 21 and 22, 1848. At the age of 19, he was the youngest graduate.[23] His Abitur certificate shows that Janknecht was a rather mediocre student.[24] However, his love for order and punctuality was especially mentioned. The best grades he earned were in Latin and History. This is all documented in his curriculum vitae. While his diligence at school was judged only satisfactory, this changed dramatically during his studies in Munster. Right after the Abitur he started to study theology in the winter semester 1848/49. During the following three semesters he attended classes in philosophy and later in theology; during this time he was acknowledged to be a very diligent student.[25] In accordance with the rule, Janknecht first had to pass a philosophy class of one to two years before he was permitted to undertake theological studies which took another four years. During this time, students were not to be enrolled in both philosophy and theology at the same time. Janknecht passed the philosophy class after one year[26] so that he was enrolled as a student of theology already in his third semester.[27] During the whole time he lived

---

[20] Schmies / Rakemann, *Spuren* 411, 459. For a detailed history of the friary and the school, see Kistenich, *Bettelmönche* 1298-1325 and 1302-1311.

[21] See the map „Die Gymnasien in Preußen im SS 1832" In: Keismann, Karl-Ernst: *Das preußische Gymnasium in Staat und Gesellschaft. Bd. 2: Höhere Bildung zwischen Reform und Reaktion 1817-1859.* (Stuttgart,) 1996, 687.

[22] Schwarz, *Festschrift* 3-87.

[23] Zu den öffentlichen Prüfungen 41; Verres, Paul: *Festschrift zur Fünfhundertjahrfeier des Städt. Gymnasiums zu Recklinghausen.*(Recklinghausen, 1929), 100.

[24] The certificate is printed in Kullmann, P. Gregor 53. There is also a copy in the personal file in ASFP Werl.

[25] See Janknecht's reports for the semesters 1848/49 and 1849/50; Universitätsarchiv Münster, Akademie B II 6 Bd. XVII, Nr. 465.

[26] Hegel, Eduard: *Geschichte der katholisch-theologischen Fakultät Münster 1773-1964. Tl. 1.* (Münster, 1966) (Münstersche Beiträge zur Theologie, 30, 1) 281, 284.

[27] Universitätsarchiv Münster, Akademie B II 6 Bd.. XVII. Nr. 465.

with the Blase family in Loerstraße[28] until he broke off his studies in Münster in the beginning of January 1850[29] in order to enter the Franciscan Order.

In contrast to other young men entering the Order, Janknecht did so after several years of studies and not right after the Abitur. The reason may have been the difficult situation in which the Order and especially the novitiate were in at that time. Furthermore, his parents did not approve of his decision. They expected their son to take up the career of a secular priest in order to repay the costs of his studies. As a member of a mendicant order he would not be able to do that. His studies must have been a heavy burden for the Janknecht family. Janknecht was allowed to defer the payment for his lessons which was only possible by producing an official certificate of financial inability to pay.[30] Finally, his parents gave their consent after a Franciscan from Dorsten wrote them a letter. The fact that it was a Franciscan from Dorsten and not from Warendorf, where the novitiate was located, hints at the basis of his relationship to the Franciscans. While his childhood was shaped by a purely Catholic and pious milieu, he formed strong connections with the Franciscans in Dorsten during college. Perhaps he already knew the Order from his childhood days in Kirchhellen. Some members of the Franciscans from Dorsten cultivated relations with Kirchhellen.[31] His experiences in Dorsten certainly had an influence on his decision to join the Franciscans rather than some other Order.[32]

[28] *Vergleichnis der Behörden, Lehrer, Beamten, Institute und sämtlicher Studierender auf der Königl. theologischen und philosophischen Akademie zu Münster im Wintersemester 1848/1849–1849/1950*, 7.

[29] He received his final report on January 5, 1850; Universitätsarchiv Münster, Akademie B II 6 Bd. XVII, Nr. 465 (Wintersemester 1849/50). Officially, the semester lasted until Palm Sunday, which was March 24 that year. Hegel, *Geschichte* 274.

[30] Universitätsarchiv Münster, Akademie B II 6 Bd. XVII, Nr. 465; Hegel, *Geschichte* 294.

[31] Büning, Heinz (Ed.): *Kirchhellen. Geschichte und Geschichten* (Kirchhellen, 1972), 316.

[32] Mathes, Joseph: *Tugendsterne Deutschlands seit der Glaubensspaltung. Ein Beitrag zur Germania Sacra.* (Steyl, 1902), 297 links Janknecht's decision to spiritual exercises that the young student attended in Freckenhorst in 1849. However, there is no proof for this theory. Indeed, there have been exercises for teachers and students in Freckenhorst on October 1849. But it cannot be determined if Janknecht participated in them. *Sonntags-Blatt für katholische Christen* 8 (1849) 704.

Since the onset of Secularization there had been severe restrictions concerning the admission of novices. It was not until 1843 that the Prussian King permitted the Saxonian Province to admit new cleric Friars other than Lay Brothers. However, the Prussian government reserved to itself the right to decide about the admissions in every single case. Thus, the first four novices were able to be invested in October 1844. In the beginning of the year 1850 the regulation that there had to be approval by the state for every single candidate was eliminated. Consequently, the Province and the Provincial for the first time in quite a long while had the sole decision-making power about the investment of novices.[33]

Theodor Janknecht was one of the first novices invested under these new circumstances. On January 17, 1850, five other men were accepted into the province. They were invested by the Guardian of the friary in Warendorf, Dionysius Epping.[34] It was the Provincial Alardus Bartscher's wish that Janknecht should be invested by P. Dionysius Epping and receive the name Gregorius.[35] Janknecht was finally invested on January 25, 1850 in Warendorf.[36] His novice master was Ignatius Jeiler. Other novices at this time were Othmar Maasmann, who later became Provincial as well;[37] Menander Gipperich, who also fulfilled important responsibilities in the leadership of the Province; and Servatius Altmicks, who became important for the mission in North America.[38] During Janknecht's last

[33] Schmies / Rakemann, *Spuren* 447, 451, 453, 461, 463, 469, 471, 477. See also Beiträge zur Geschichte des Noviziates der Sächsischen Franziskanerprovinz vom hl. Kreuz. Zur Hundertjahrfeier der Eröffnung des Noviziates in Warendorf am 4. Oktober 1844. In: *Vita Seraphica* 25 (1944) 147-164. Kordwittenborg, Hans-Ulrich: Die Sächsische Franziskanerprovinz vom Hl. Kreuz in der zweiten Hälfte des 19. Jahrhunderts. In: *100 Jahre Franziskaner in Dortmund.* (Werl,) 1995, 31-45.

[34] OFM Klosterarchiv Warendorf, III. Fach 28 Nr. 3. Schematismus Provinciae Saxoniae S. Crucis Ordinis FF. Minorum S.P.N. Francisci Recollectorum. In: *Compendium Chronologicum Provinciae Saxoniae S. Crucis Ordinis Fratrum Minorum S. Franisci Recollectorum.* (Warendorf, 1873), 26.

[35] Bartscher wrote to Epping on January 19: "Charissime Confrater! Please invest the student Janknecht and give him the name Gregorius"; OFM Klosterarchiv Warendorf, III. Fach 28 Nr. 3.

[36] Schematismus 1873, 26.

[37] Becherer, Heike: Othmar Maasmann. In: *Management und Minoritas. Lebensbilder Sächsischer Franziskanerprovinziale vom 13. bis zum 20 Jahrhundert.* Dieter Berg (Ed.). (Kevelear, 2003)

[38] Schematismus 1873, 26.

weeks in the novitiate there was also Aloysius Lauer, from the Thuringian Province who would later become General.[39] According to his obituary in the necrology, Janknecht stood out in the novitiate "by honesty, tender piety and diligence in the religious life."[40] His novitiate lasted the canonical "year and a day" so that Janknecht could make his profession on January 26, 1851.[41] Then he went to Paderborn to continue his studies. Since the Order's theological studies did not resume until 1861, the students attended the academy of Paderborn.[42] Vicar General Boekamp wrote to the Guardian of Paderborn, Bonifatius Ostendorf, on February 24, 1853, that the bishop had decided to admit Frater Gregorius Janknecht to presbyteral ordination.[43] He received Holy Orders on March 7, 1853 in the Cathedral of Paderborn.[44]

There had been efforts to bring back the Franciscans to Dusseldorf for a number of years. After the most important preparations were finished, the first Friars could move into the provisional building in July 1853. It seems that Janknecht was one of these Friars. He appears on the list of Friars in the Dusseldorf friary on September 20, 1853, together with the two Paters Bernhard Horn and Leonhardt Gehlen as well as two Lay Brothers.[45]

---

[39] Since Thuringia did not run a novitiate in the middle of the 19th century, the novices were sent to Warendorf for their formation after 1850. *Beiträge zur Geschichte des Noviziates* 157f. Also Enneking, Nicopherus: Pater Aloys Lauer. Leben und Wirken des ersten deutschen Generalministers des Franziskanerordens. In: *Thuringia Franciscana NF* 34 (1979) 491-508; NF 35 (1980) 275-294, 423-476, NF 36 (1891) 111-127, 237-269. There was a friendship between Janknecht and Lauer which stems from this time. It was Lauer who wrote Janknecht's obituary in the *Acta Ordinis Minorum*; Enneking, Pater Aloys Lauer (passim) und NF 35 (1890) 287, 293. There are also letters from Janknecht to Lauer in the years 1856-1858 in the archives of the Thuringia Province in Fulda.

[40] Translation of the *Acta Ordinis Minorum* 15 (1896) 60 in Loddenkötter, P. Gregor 212.

[41] Schematismus 1891, 1.

[42] *Festschrift zum 300 jährigen Bestehen des Franziskanerklosters Paderborn 1658-1958.* (Werl, 1958), 276f.

[43] OFM Klosterarchiv Paderborn, Best. A, Nr. 216. Also in Loddenkötter, P. Gregor 212.

[44] Schematismus 1873, 26.

[45] Schmitz, Cajetan: Gründung des Franziskanerklosters in Düsseldorf. In: *Jahrbuch der Sächsischen Franziskanerprovinz vom Heiligen Kreuze.* (Düsseldorf, 1907), 83-111.

During Janknecht's residence in Dusseldorf, the Province decided to establish a course of Humanistic studies in Wiedenbrück. Janknecht was supposed to teach there as a junior university professor. In order to fill this post, he had to study classic philology. For this purpose he went to Munster in the fall of 1853 and enrolled in the philosophy program there.[46] Now he did not have to rent a room from an unknown landlord as he did at the beginning of his studies; now he could live in the new residence which was set up that year. The residence was located at the Horsteberg next to the cathedral and it was the apartment intended for the cathedral's Father Confessor.[47]

Janknecht pursued his studies in classic philology with great zeal. Consequently, he received good grades without exception.[48] He interrupted his studies only reluctantly in the summer of 1854, when he was elected *Lector philologiae fratrum clericorum* for the Warendorf friary on June 8, 1854. The lack of members, especially capable teachers, forced the Province to change its plans for Janknecht on short notice. Thus the young Franciscan had to ask the professors again for a performance report before the semester's official end—just as he had done four years previously.[49] There is a special remark on his report.[50]

Janknecht did not serve long as a junior professor in Warendorf. One year later, on September 1855, the Provincial Chapter in Wiedenbrück elected him Provincial of the Saxonian Province of Franciscans by an absolute majority.[51] By this time he was not even 26 years old and had not even been a member of the Order for six years. He had been a priest for only two and a half years. The reason for the election of such a young and inexperienced man as Provincial was the relatively small number of candidates that the Province had

[46] Verzeichnis der Behörden WS 1853/1854, 8.

[47] Ewert, Regina: Geschichte des Franziskanerordens „Zu der Heiligen Maria von den Engeln" zu Münster. In: *Vita Seraphica* 53 (1972) 129-155 as well as Bockholt, Berthold: *Die Orden des heiligen Franziskus in Münster 1917*, 48; *Verzeichnis der Behörden WS 1853/1854*, 8.

[48] Universitätsarchiv Münster, Akademie B II 6 Bd. XX, Nr. 34 (WS 1853/1854) and SS 1854.

[49] Universitätsarchiv Münster, Akademie B II 6 Bd. XX, Nr. 34 (WS 1853/1854).

[50] Universitätsarchiv Münster, Akademie B II 6 Bd. XX, Nr. 34 (SS 1854).

[51] Besides Janknecht, Othmar Massmann, Maximilian Kirchner and Xaverius Kaufmann ran for election. Janknecht gained seven votes, the others one each. ASFP Werl, Acta capitularia 1843-1888, 141, 149.

at its disposal. By 1855 the Saxonian Province counted only 47 Paters.[52] Those who had entered the Order before the Secularization were too old to serve as Provincial. Furthermore, their idea of life in the Order greatly differed from that of the younger generation. Thus, Xaverius Kaufmann's election as Provincial in 1852 had already marked a generational change in the leadership of the Province[53] which also took into account the Alcantarine Movement.[54]

2. Provincial from 1855 until 1861

The situation in the Saxonian Province was uneasy when P. Gregory Janknecht took over its leadership. The province had slowly begun to recover from the set-backs it experienced during secularization, especially the reduction in personnel. The separation from the Alcantarines had cost the province further manpower. On the one hand many young friars, especially young priests had left the Order. On the other hand the situation had led to quarrels between the generations. Janknecht's first circular letter dated September 29, 1855 clearly showed his awareness of the problems which such a situation could cause for a young Provincial and that he was determined to prevent them from the very beginning.[55] At the same time he was convinced that a stricter observance of the rule was absolutely necessary.[56] In contrast to the Alcantarines, he saw the province's future in a reformed

---

[52] ASFP Werl, tables of the Chapter 1855, Loddenkötter, P. Gregor 110.

[53] Xaverius Kaufmann had been one of the first four novices after the Secularization who were invested on October 3, 1844. He was born on October 7, 1825 and was ordained on November 30, 1847. See: Schematismus 1873, 25. At his election, he was 27 years old and a member of the Order for eight years.

[54] For further information: Reinhold, Julius: Die Alkantarinerbewegung in der Sächsischen Franziskanerprovinz vom Hl. Kreuz. In: *Vita Seraphica* 30 (1949) 45-62, 154-176, 221-247.

[55] ASFP Werl, Rundschreiben, Gregor Janknecht 1855-1861 (Wiedenbrück, 29. September 1855). The circular is a German translation of a Latin circular from Sept. 28, 1855. Circulars were generally written in Latin and later translated into German so that the lay brothers could also understand the instructions. Fleckenstein, Gisela: *Die Franziskaner im Rheinland 1875-1918.* (Werl, 1992) (Franziskanische Forschungen 39), 143.

[56] He had criticized the conditions in the province already earlier. In the fall of 1850 he had written a letter to the General in favor of a strict observance together with other novices. Reinhold, Alkantarinerbewegung, 55.

Saxonia rather than in a separation from the province. Thus he wrote at the beginning of his term of office as Provincial: *"I regard it as my duty to admonish the brothers to the pure and full observance of the rule which we have promised God. On the other hand I will remove every obstacle to the pure observance by issuing appropriate orders."*[57] Reforms of that kind would only succeed if the disputes among the brothers could be settled. Consequently, he tried to intervene as a mediator with his circular and attempted to create an understanding among the younger Friars for the older members of the Province.[58] The first circular contained the issues that were paramount for Janknecht. They were the basis for his entire later work in Saxonia and other Provinces.[59]

During his first year as Provincial, Janknecht repeatedly had to deal with the Alcantarines. As much as he advocated sympathy for the older Friars in the Province, he also engaged himself on behalf of former Alcantarines who returned to Saxonia and lived there under stricter conditions.[60] Usually two were placed together. They lived on their own in separate friaries and were not allowed to have contact with the other Friars except for the Guardians. They were excluded from the sacraments and the celebration of the Mass. This regulation stemmed from the previous Provincial, Xaverius Kaufmann, and Janknecht saw no reason for revoking it,[61] as he explicitly wrote to Bishop Drepper from Paderborn.[62] Janknecht abolished that restriction in his province only after the Bishop from Münster had allowed the Alcantarines the reception of communion in February 1856. Only three regulations remained in force. First the Alcantarines could only receive and send letters that were read by the Guardians beforehand. Secondly, they were not allowed to have contact with lay people without permission of the Guardians. Finally, all the Friars were prohibited to talk to the former Alcantarines about the Rule.[63]

---

[57] ASFP Werl, Rundschreiben, Gregor Janknecht 1855-1861 (Wiedenbrück, 29. September 1855).

[58] ASFP Wer, Gregor Janknecht 1855-1861 (Wiedenbrück, 29. September 1855).

[59] Loddenkötter, P. Gregor 213.

[60] EBA Paderborn, Acta generalia Bd. XIII Nr. 5, fol. 179r+v; EBA Paderborn, Acta generalia Bd. XIII Nr. 5, fol. 183r+v.

[61] Reinhold, Alcantarinbewegung 224f.

[62] EBA Paderborn, Acta generalia Bd. XIII Nr. 5, fol. 179r+v.

[63] ASFP Werl, Rundschreiben, Gregor Janknecht 1855-1861 (Wiedenbrück, 25. Februar 1856). See also: Reinhold, Alkantarinbewegung 225.

In the fall of 1856 Janknecht was instructed by the General to incorporate into the Province all the Alcantarines living in Saxonia. The Alcantarine case came to a conclusion in 1861 when Janknecht brought back into the Saxonian Province the two Alcantarines Ignatius Jeiler and Antonius Pommer assisted by the mediation of the Bishop of Münster. The two Friars were living in Rome by that time and the Pope had reserved to himself the decision about them.[64]

During his first term Janknecht was constantly working on the renewal of the Saxonian Province. At the same time he was profiting by the general development of the whole Order. In 1856 there was the first General Chapter since 1768 in which all Provinces took part. At first, the political conditions hindered a meeting of all representatives of the Order. Later, internal complications in the Order prevented a meeting of the whole Order. However, in 1856 General Venantius of Celano summoned a Chapter of the entire Order, which was to take place in Rome under the Pope's chairmanship.[65] Since the General had repeatedly denounced the faulty discipline in many Provinces of the Order, Janknecht had great hopes for the Chapter.[66] Thus, he participated in it as a Provincial.[67]

In preparation for the General Chapter, there were several important tasks that all of the Provinces, including Saxonia, needed to complete before the Chapter began. The last status report of the Order had been drawn up at the last Chapter in 1768. The General intended to compile a new status report at the Chapter in 1856. This status report would include not only information about the friaries, the Friars, and studies but also detailed information about the Second and Third Orders and all Guardians' reports of the individual convents. Consequently the General asked the provinces to assemble this information before the beginning of the Chapter. Janknecht forwarded this instruction to the Guardians who had to prepare these lists. For a task like this, a well-kept archive would

---

[64] Giesenbrock, P. Gregor 6.

[65] Holzapfel, Heribert: *Handbuch der Geschichte des Franziskanerordens.* (Freiburg/Br., 1909), 371.

[66] ASFP Werl. Rundschreiben, Gregor Janknecht 1855-1861 (Wiedenbrück, 15. Januar 1856).

[67] *Capitulum Generale totius Ordinis Fratrum Minorum S.P.N. Francisci Romae habitum in Templo S. Mariae de Aracoeli die 10 Maji 1856.* (Rome, 1857), here 19, Nr. 104.

have been helpful, but such was rarely the case. In order to simplify the administration of the Province, Janknecht introduced the job of house archivist.[68] Jankecht had a high regard for well-kept archives, since he frequently depended on documents from previous times during his term as Provincial. In many places the presence of the Franciscans had been interrupted by secularization. Consequently, there were frequently questions concerning the Friars' rights and duties because these were unclear.[69] Janknecht was very interested in an overview of all the important facts and proceedings of the Province and its friaries. This explains a manuscript in the General's archive in Rome.[70] This *Historia Provinciae S. Crucis* from 1862 must be the result of longstanding efforts to gather all important information about the Province which were relevant in 1862. Its four volumes contain all the data that the General had required for the General Chapter in 1856. Perhaps the endeavor could not be finished in time due to the difficult circumstances. Or perhaps the results did not satisfy Janknecht. In any case the work was continued and finished in 1862—right before the next General Chapter. The document was signed by the current Provincial Maasmann, the two former Provincials Kaufmann and Janknecht, Custodian Rüter as well as the four Definitors Orbach, Menke, Wessendorf and Ostendorf.[71] Janknecht's efforts were continued when the first printed *Schematismus* of the Saxony Province was published in 1873. The *Schematismus* was introduced by a history of the Province, of the individual convents, and a list of all Provincials since 1628.[72]

The first years of the restoration of the Province would clearly show Janknecht's interest in proven traditions and the history of the Province. This would influence his actions and decisions throughout

---

[68] ASFP Werl. Rundschreiben, Gregor Janknecht 1855-1861 (Wiedenbrück, 15. Januar 1856).

[69] This was the case for the teachers at the different schools run by the Franciscans before the secularization.

[70] AG OFM Rom, C 40 (Historia Provinciae S. Crucis). By now, there is a copy in the archive in the ASFP Werl.

[71] See the last page of the individual chapters.

[72] Schematismus 1873 as well as *Compendium Chronologicum Provinciae Saxoniae S. Crucis Ordinis Fratrum Minorum S. Francisci Recollectorum.* (Warendorf, 1873); see also: Reinhold, Korrespondez 48.

his entire life. In official letters to the friars he often referred to Saxonia's successful past. That is how he tried to strengthen their awareness of and interest in it.[73] Perhaps in that way he hoped to cultivate in the present Friars a desire to follow the good example of Friars of earlier times.

This special fondness of Janknecht may also be the reason why he reinstituted the old statutes of the Province from 1735.[74] He achieved that at the mid-term chapter in Wiedenbrück in March 1857. The Definitorium revised the old statutes and adjusted them where necessary. The ceremonies were also revised. Janknecht informed the friars about the innovations—especially in the daily schedule—in his circular letter of March 21, 1857.[75] He notified Procurator Bernard van Loo about these measures in a letter dated March 28, 1857.[76] After the next Chapter in 1858 he pointed out in another circular that the statutes from 1735 with their corresponding adjustments had to be observed.[77] Janknecht had already distributed the revised statutes in a circular letter in January 1858.[78] Moreover, he participated in the first Chapter of the Thuringian Custody, whose main focus was on new statutes for the Province. Finally, it was decided in Fulda to reinstitute the old statutes of the Thuringian Province dating back to 1676.[79] The almost parallel development concerning the statutes of the province as well as Janknecht's presence at the Thuringian Chapter allow the conclusion that the Saxon Provincial had profoundly influenced the direction of the Thuringian custody.

---

[73] ASFP Werl, Rundschreiben, Gregor Janknecht 1855-1861 (Wiedenbrück, 29. September 1855); Kullmann, P. Gregor 99.

[74] *Statuta Provincialia almae Provinciae Saxoniae C. Crucis. Ordinis Fratrum Minorum S. Francisci Strictoris Observantiae. Revisa, Aucta, emendata, & recepta à toto Capitulo Provinciali, celebrato in Conventu Monasteriensi ad S. Antonium Paduam.* (Münster, 1735).

[75] ASFP Werl, Rundschreiben, Gregor Janknecht 1855-1861 (Warendorf, 21. März 1857).

[76] AG OFM ROM, SA 29 fol. 78r+v.

[77] ASFP Werl, Rundschreiben, Gregor Janknecht 1855-1861 (Warendorf, 10. September 1858).

[78] ASFP Werl, Rundschreiben, Gregor Janknecht 1855-1861 (Warendorf, 30. Januar 1858)

[79] Enneking, Pater Aloys Lauer NF 35 (1980) 459.

Besides his position as Provincial Janknecht was also elected Master of Novices at the mid-term chapter in Wiedenbrück.[80] Since the Provincial's office and the novitiate were in Warendorf at that time, such a co-mingling of responsibilities in one person was theoretically possible. However, the two offices were probably not permanently compatible due to the amount of time each office required. When Janknecht was confirmed as Provincial at the next Chapter on July 21, 1858 in Wiedenbrück, Mathias Hiltermann was appointed as Master of Novices.[81] Janknecht had probably fulfilled the Definitorium's expectations which resulted in his re-election. The election result was quite clear: he received 10 out of 13 votes right away on the first ballot.[82] Consequently he appeared to have more self-confidence. Even though his next circular letter after the Chapter started with the usual humble clichés, he used it to portray the success of his previous work. He quotes a letter from the procurator Bernard van Loo in which he explicitly praises the state of the Saxonian Province. Furthermore, the Pope had personally promised him every support. This is how the Provincial attempted to undermine the influence of his critics.[83]

The Province had erected a new friary during Janknecht's first term. The church and the grounds on top of Mount Apollinaris were donated by Baron Franz Egon von Fürstenberg-Stammheim. The Baron wished that this famous place of pilgrimage would be looked after by the Franciscans. For this reason he contacted the Guardian of the friary in Hardenberg-Neviges, Xaverius Kaufmann. The Saxonian Province was already maintaining a place of pilgrimage there. The two men finally persuaded Janknecht of this idea. Thus, the new friary in Remagen was accepted at the mid-term chapter in Wiedenbrück in March. The first Saxonian Franciscans moved into the residence on March 24th with P. Xaverius Kaufmann as Guardian.[84]

---

[80] ASFP Werl, Acta capitularia 1843-1888, 163; also Peters, Benedikt: *Totenbuch der Sächsischen Franziskanerprovinz vom Heiligen Kreuz. 2. Bd und Ergänzungsband,* (Werl, 1947-1954), II, 50 and 263.

[81] Peters, *Totenbuch II,* 263; Kullmann, P. Gregor 55.

[82] ASFP Werl, Acta capitularia 1843-1888, 179, 189.

[83] ASFP Werl, Rundschreiben, Gregor Janknecht 1855-1861 (Warendorf, 10. September 1858).

[84] *100 Jahre Franziskaner auf dem Apollinarisberg in Remagen* (Remagen, 1957), 31f. Also Schmies / Rakemann, *Spuren* 479.

After Janknecht's re-election, the Province could accept other new residences. At the request of the Prince Bishop of Breslau, Saxonia took over the pastoral care of the pilgrims at St. Annaberg in Silesia in 1859. Previously, the Alcantarines had served there. Janknecht had initially refused the bishop's request due to personnel constraints. On the one hand, the number of Friars was rising, but was still not sufficient to staff all of the friaries. On the other hand, pastoral care of people in Upper Silesia required Polish-speaking priests, who were not available in Saxonia. The Prince Bishop promised to leave the Polish-speaking priest who was currently serving at the place of pilgrimage.[85] Thus the care of St. Annaberg was accepted at the Chapter in Wiedenbrück in July 1858. At first there were some complications in the maintenance of the place. After intervention, on-site visits and discussions with the Prince Bishop, the first Saxon Franciscans arrived at St. Annaberg in August 1859. A second novitiate was founded there in 1860 in order to promote Polish-speaking vocations and to solve the language problem.[86] However, that novitiate was closed in 1863.[87]

In 1860 the residences in Munster, Aachen and on the Hülfensberg were established. There had already been a small community in Munster close to the cathedral since 1853.[88] But the bishop as well as the citizens of Munster wished the pastoral care of the Franciscans to be intensified. Consequently the leadership of the Province was repeatedly asked to expand the presence of Franciscans in Munster. At first, this wish could not be granted because of the lack of Friars. However, in 1858 Janknecht promised the bishop to increase the Franciscan presence in Munster. The Provincial Chapter in 1858 decided to build a new convent. After the Province had

---

[85] On February 6, 1858, Janknecht told procurator Bernard van Loo about the repeated requests to take over St. Annaberg in Silesia. Reinhold, Alkantarinerbewegung 247.

[86] Beiträge zur Geschichte des Noviziates 163f.

[87] Reisch, Chrysogonus: *Geschichte des St. Annaberges in Oberschlesien.* (Breslau, 1910), 354-364. See also Teichmann, Lucius: Schlesisches Klosterbuch. St. Annaberg Franziskanerkloster. In: *Jahrbuch der schlesischen Friedrich-Wilhelms-Universität zu Breslau 30* (1989) 30-43. The takeover of St. Annaberg was the basis for the foundation of the Silesian custody in 1902 which was erected as an independent province in 1911. Schmies / Rakemann, *Spuren* 527, 535.

[88] Ewert, Geschichte 136-138 as well as Bockholt, *Orden* 48.

obtained enough money and acquired the land, the construction could start at Hörsterplatz in 1860. The first set of plans called for a spacious convent. These plans were rejected by the leadership of the Province. Financial considerations may have played an important role. The province, and especially Janknecht, were anxious to observe the rule of poverty more rigorously at this time. In 1857 Janknecht had vehemently denied permission for decorations at the back of the new convent in Dusseldorf—even though it was required by the Royal Police Administration. Consequently, a second modified building plan was finally constructed in Munster.[89]

There had been a similar situation in Aachen. The existing Franciscan convent had been closed down during secularization. In the middle of the 19th century there were several movements to bring the Franciscans back into town. This was strongly urged by the foundress of the Poor Sisters of St. Francis, Franziska Schervier. She hoped that the young community would be supervised by the Franciscans. The members of the Saxonian Province seemed best suited due to their strict observance.[90] However, the province was at first not willing to burden the weak Saxonia with another residence. Later, the plan failed because of the resistance of the Aachen clergy and the government respectively. Nevertheless, Franziska Schervier continued her endeavors. Finally she and Johannes Höver, founder of the Community of the Poor Brothers of St. Francis, succeeded in persuading two Aachen citizens to donate a piece of land to the Franciscans. Thus, the Franciscans were able to move into their new residence in 1860.[91]

After Remagen, St. Annaberg and Munster, the Saxonian Province received another plea from Eichsfeld (a region of Thuringia). In this case the Friars were supposed to maintain the place of pilgrimage at Mount Hülfensberg. Already in 1846 Provincial Alardus Bartscher had been asked to send brothers. Due to insufficient personnel the request could neither then nor during the following years be granted.

---

[89] Schmitz, Gründung 109.

[90] Gammersbach, Suitbert: Franziska Schervier (1819-1876). Schwester und Helferin der Minderbrüder in Aachen. In: *Rhenania Franciscana* 42 (1989) 230-240.

[91] Clasen, *Hundert Jahre* 9-11; also Jeiler, Ignatius: *Die gottselige Mutter Franziska Schervier. Stifterin der Genossenschaft der Armenschwestern vom h. Franziskus.* (Freiburg/Br., 1927), 257-259.

Eventually the Definitorium had to reject the request in 1857. As a result, Bishop Konrad Martin of Paderborn brought himself into the negotiations. Since he himself was originally from Geismar next to Hülfensberg, he had a strong personal interest in bringing the Franciscans there.[92] In March 1860 he was finally successful and received Janknecht's promise. However, Hülfensberg was originally intended by the Province as an interim solution until permission for a residence in Hagis, another town in the Eichsfeld, could be obtained. This permission was never granted so that Janknecht intended to withdraw the Friars living on Mount Hülfensberg. Again it was the Bishop who persuaded them to stay permanently at Mount Hülfensberg.[93]

By comparing the establishment of the different residences, it can be noted that the course of events was always similar. The Province or the Provincial was always approached with a request to establish a new Franciscan convent. The initiative never came from the Province itself. On the contrary, the requests were all rejected due to lack of personnel, regardless of who the Provincial was at that time. There had been requests for almost all the convents mentioned above before Janknecht took office. But Alardus Bartscher as well as Xaverius Kaufmann were both unable to staff new residences because of insufficient personnel resources. Still Kaufmann was upbeat about the extension of the Province. This was evident in the foundation of the convent in Dusseldorf during his term and the acceptance of the convent on Mount Apollinaris in Remagen. In the 1850s the personnel situation started to ease gradually so that new residences could be established. This was not so much because of Janknecht's efforts but rather a logical conclusion of Saxonia's enormous growth due to the improved political condition and the increasing number of novices. A close look at the new foundations will reveal that Janknecht's personal attitude toward the establishment of these new

---

[92] Konrad Martin cultivated close relations with the Franciscans. Brandt, Hans-Jürgen / Hengst, Karl: *Die Bischöfe und Erzbischöfe von Paderborn.* (Paderborn, 1984), 304-312; also Fleckenstein, Gisela: Reaktionen der rheinischen Franziskaner auf die Kulturkampfgesetzgebung. In: *Rottenburger Jahrbuch für Kirchengeschichte* 15 (1996) 149-157; Schmies / Rakemann, *Spuren* 517, 555.

[93] *Der Hülfensberg und Bebendorf.* o.O. o.J. (1900), 14; also Opfermann, Bernhard: *Die Klöster des Eichsfeldes in ihrer Geschichte.* (Heiligenstadt, 1961) (ND 1998) 205.

convents was rather negative. The persuasion of influential persons was usually necessary to convince him to establish a new residence.

The residence in Dusseldorf became a convent at the mid-term chapter in Wiedenbrück in September 1859. At the same time it became the place for the theological studies and the Provincial's office moved there from Warendorf, since Janknecht became Guardian of the convent in addition to his role as Provincial.[94]

In the following spring a Provincial Chapter took place in Cologne at the initiative of Archbishop Geissel. Its topics and directions were similar to what would be evident at Vatican I a decade later.[95] Gregory Janknecht participated in this assembly as a representative of the Order subject to the authority of the Holy See.[96]

3. The Mission in North America[97]

Throughout his life Gregory Janknecht was especially interested in the missions. He intended to go into the Chinese mission after his ordination as priest, but this was impossible at first owing to the shortage of staff in Saxonia and later because he was elected Provincial.[98] Therefore it was with great pleasure that he accepted the

[94] ASFP Werl, Acta capitularia 1843-1888 199, 204. Peters, *Totenbuch* II, 293. Until 1897 the Provincial's office always moved the Provincial's place of residence. See: Fleckenstein, Gisela: Reaktionen der rheinischen Franziskaner auf die Kulturkampfgesetzgebung. In: *Rottenburger Jahrbuch für Kirchengeschichte* 15 (1996) 149-157; Schmies / Rakemann, *Spuren* 517, 555.

[95] Trippen, Norbert: Die katholischen Fakultäten Deutschlands im 19. Jahrhundert zwischen staatlichem Anspruch und kirchlichem Mißtrauen. In: Lill, Rudolf / Traniello, Francesco (Ed.): *Der Kulturkampf in Italien und in den deutschen Ländern.* (Berlin, 1993) (Schriften des Italienisch-Deutschen Historischen Instituts in Trient, 5) 299-320. Schatz, Klaus: Das Erste Vatikanum. In Weitlauff, Manfred (Ed.): *Kirche im 19. Jahrhundert.* (Regensburg, 1998), 140-162.

[96] Hegel, Eduard: *Das Erzbistum Köln zwischen der Restauration des 19. Jahrhunderts und der Restauration des 20. Jahrhunderts 1815-1962.* (Köln,) 1987 (Geschichte des Erzbistums Köln 5) 179.

[97] The chapters about the missions in North America and Brazil can only be given a short overview in this essay. There will be a more detailed study about these topics in the volume about the missions in the History of the Province which will be published in 2006, edited by Dieter Berg.

[98] Griesenbrock, P. Gregor 4; Kullmann, P. Gregor 54; Loddenkötter, P. Gregor 224. The following description is based on Habig, Marion A.: *Heralds of the King. The Franciscans of the St. Louis-Chicago Province 1858-1958.* (Chicago,) 1958, 25-175.

offer of the Bishop of Alton, Illinois, Henry Damian Juncker, in 1858 to found a Franciscan friary in his diocese. The principal aim was to counteract the lack of priests in this area and, furthermore, to create a base for future missionary work. The American bishop had come to Europe especially to deal with this issue. Bishop Konrad Martin referred his colleague to Gregory Janknecht, whom he met soon afterwards in the friary of Paderborn. In a letter of recommendation dated March 15, 1858, Bishop Martin wrote to Janknecht: *"Thus, I repeat my request and ask you also in the name of my honored brother: If it is possible, have mercy upon him and his poor diocese."*[99] Janknecht, who had an extremely positive attitude towards the issue, had to wait for the Definitorium and the General to agree. On April 22 he was able to inform Bishop Juncker about the Definitorium's positive decision of April 21, 1858, and to let him know that two priests would be sent to the new residence. At the same time he asked the bishop to consult the General personally concerning this issue in order to speed up the proceedings. On May 18, Janknecht himself wrote to the General and—with reference to the unanimous decision of the Definitorium—asked for permission to fulfill the wish of the American bishop.[100] Thus the first nine members of the Province were able to leave for North America from Warendorf on August 24, 1858.[101] Gregory Janknecht made sure that the travel expenses were refunded by the *Leopoldinenstiftung* in Vienna.

The ship which carried the group across the Atlantic from Bremerhaven reached New York on September 14. From there the Franciscans continued their journey by train to Alton, Illinois and finally to their first ministerial site in Teutopolis. On October 2 they officially took charge of the spiritual care of the community there, which consisted primarily of German immigrants. Although they began their pastoral work under extremely difficult conditions, it

---

[99] See: ZUM GOLDENEN JUBILÄUM der Provincia SS. Cordis Jesu. In: *Vita Seraphica* 10 (1929) 49-52.

[100] Schmitz, Cajetan, Zum Jubilaeum der Ordensprovinz vom Heiligsten Herzen Jesu in Nordamerika. In: *Beitraege zur Geschichte der Saechsischen Franziskanerprovinz vom Heiligen Kreuze I.* (1908), 98: Jubiläum 98; ZUM GOLDENEN JUBILÄUM 50.

[101] The group consisted of three priests: Damian Hennewig, Johannes Kapistran Zwinge and Servatius Altmicks, four Lay Brothers: Irenäus Drewes, Paschalis Kutsche, Marianus Beile and Julius Schmänck as well as two Tertiaries: Edmund Wilde and Franziskus Uphoff; Habig, *Heralds* 28f.

extended to the surrounding areas within a few weeks. Two of the three priests traveled about to perform missionary work among the people and to provide them with the sacraments as often as possible. Because the Franciscans had to travel great distances on roads which were in extremely bad condition, Janknecht decided in 1859 to request that the American Friars be allowed to wear secular clothes during their journey and use money if absolutely necessary. These dispensations were granted on July 31.[102]

Soon the Franciscans were asked to establish a permanent residence at Quincy which at that time was the biggest city of the Diocese of Alton. Bishop Junker also asked the Franciscans to establish a grammar school there. Janknecht, as a Provincial, must have been very pleased to give permission for this project since attracting new candidates to the Order was always of major importance to him. This is also reflected in the decision of the Provincial leaders to send a second group of Friars to North America, which was done on September 25, 1859. After these six new missionaries had arrived in Teutopolis on November 26, 1859, the new house could be opened a few days later. The following year, Janknecht came to the North American mission for his first canonical visitation. He left Dusseldorf together with the Provincial Secretary, Kilian Schlösser, and Brother Robert Michel. They reached New York during the night between August 6-7 and continued by train to Cincinnati. They stayed with the Franciscans of the Custody of St. John the Baptist which had grown out of the mission of the American Province St. Leopold the year before. Janknecht also talked to Bishop Junker about the two

---

[102] Hardick, Lothar: Zum hundertjährigen Bestehen der Ordensprovinz vom Heiligsten Herzen Jesu in Nordamerika. In: *Spiritualität und Geschichte. Festgabe für LotharHardick OFM.* Ed.: Dieter Berg. (Werl, 1993) (Saxonia Franciscana, 2), 157-161;Schmitz, Jubiläum 104. A letter from Servatius Altmicks to Janknecht from May 11, 1859 gives detailed insights into the daily routine of the missionaries: „*Eben das Reiten ist in solchen Fällen eine unumgängliche Nothwendigkeit, da wir oft Wege haben, die man nicht mal im Tage, viel weniger in der Nacht passieren kann. Mit dem Wagen, da oft kaum ein gutes Reitpferd sich mit Mühe durcharbeitet, ist es nicht möglich. Dies ist übrigens hier, wo fast jedes Frauenzimmer reiten kann und muß, gar nicht auffallend. Wir müssen dann freilich, der Ehrbarkeit wegen, statt unsers gewöhnlichen Femorals, eine dunkelfarbige Reithose anlegen (der Habit aufgeschürzt), und steigen wir ab, so wird der Habit abgelassen, und der Mönch ist vollständig fertig.*" Ein Brief Aus Amerika. In: *Katholisches Missionsblatt* 9 (1860) 5f., 23-25, 30-32.

houses of the Saxonian Franciscans in the Diocese of Alton before he and his companions continued to Teutopolis, where they arrived on August 18. Janknecht then carried out the visitation of both houses. When he returned to Teutopolis the Bishop was waiting to discuss an important new project with him. He wanted the Franciscans to establish and administer a college for boys as well as a seminary of the Diocese for Catholic priests. In spite of the persistent problems of the Province in Germany, Janknecht agreed to support the project and provide additional qualified staff. As early as 1862, St. John's College was opened as the Seminary of the Diocese of Alton.[103]

In order to recruit new candidates for the Order in their new area, Janknecht named Kilian Master of Novices and thus opened the first novitiate of the mission in Teutopolis. On October 4, shortly before his departure, he personally invested Brother Edmund Wildes with the habit of the First Order and admitted local resident Henry Heuer as Brother Joseph to the Third Order. On October 7 Janknecht directed a circular letter to the friaries in Teutopolis and Quincy in which he granted Ferdinand Bergmeyer the authority to act as a Provincial would in all tasks concerning personnel changes. His circular letter to the Saxonian Province from November 29, 1860, reflects his extremely positive attitude towards the conditions and customs of the missionaries he observed during his stay in America.[104]

The authorization of Ferdinand Bergmeyer as acting Provincial was the first step towards creating an independent mission. When Othmar Maasmann took over from Janknecht as Provincial in 1861 he intended to organize the mission into an independent custody. For this reason, he wanted to send Janknecht and several other brothers to North America to put everything in order. In his letter to Damian Hennewig from April 4, 1862, he especially emphasized that, strictly speaking, Janknecht was indispensable to Saxonia at the time, but that this sacrifice had to be made for a couple of months.[105]

---

[103] Schmies/Rakemann, *Spuren* 483. For the history of the St. Joseph's College during its first years, see Hagedorn, Eugenius: *Beiträge zur Geschichte von Teutopolis und Umgegend unter besonderer Berücksichtigung des Wirkens der dortigen Franziskaner.* (St. Louis, 1902), 74-88.

[104] There is an English translation of the circular in Habig, 59.

[105] Habig, *Heralds* 79. The original is located in the Archives of the Sacred Heart Province in St. Louis.

However, his plan was not put into practice as Janknecht could indeed not be spared from Germany at that very moment. Instead, the Master of Novices, Matthias Hiltermann, was sent to America as the Commissary Provincial and Janknecht took over from him as Master of Novices. With Hiltermann's arrival on July 19, 1862, the American mission was made an independent Commissionary and thus was able to make decisions more autonomously. Nevertheless, Maasmann continued to pursue his aim of converting the mission into an independent custody as soon as possible, as he considered it impossible to oversee American concerns from Germany on a long term basis. The Friars in America, however, rejected this proposal, pointing out that the mission was in the difficult period of its initial stages and thus such a step would be asking too much of them, Maasmann consequently refrained from his demand. In 1864 Kilian Schlösser became Commissary of the mission in America. After Janknecht had been elected Provincial again in 1867, he confirmed his former secretary in that office. Early in 1869, however, Schlösser asked the Provincial to accept his resignation. Janknecht, who showed great understanding for his decision in his letter to Schlösser, announced another personal journey to North America. On September 23, 1869, Janknecht left Dusseldorf together with nine other missionaries. They reached Teutopolis on October 9. First Janknecht carried out the canonical visitation of the mission. Afterwards he arranged a meeting with the elderly friars on November 10 at which the question of establishing a custody which would be largely independent of the Mother Province was again brought up for discussion. Although once again this idea was not embraced or accepted,[106] a new Commissioner, Mauritius Klostermann, was appointed and six discreets were elected to support the Commissary in his decisions. The Commissary was not only authorized to transfer Friars to other residences, he could also proclaim official decrees.

In a circular letter dated December 26, 1869 Janknecht outlined some rules of conduct for teachers, priests, and missionaries. Shortly before his return to Germany on January 26, 1870, he gave his last instructions from Cleveland in a letter to the new Commissioner on

---

[106] Even the General judged this endeavor as too early and suggested that the current situation should be in effect for at least for three more years. Habig, *Heralds* 96f.

January 20, 1870. On February 8 he reached Wiedenbrück after an absence of four and a half months.

As the conditions of the *Kulturkampf* began to affect Saxonia more and more after 1872, Janknecht wrote to Commissary Klostermann on May 29, 1873. In his letter he enumerated all the Commissary's rights and confirmed them once again in order to prevent misunderstandings. In doing so, Janknecht largely extended the power of the commissariat. Owing to the situation in Germany, which was rather insecure, he probably intended to make the convents in North America as independent as possible from those in the Mother Province. Nevertheless, several problems arose which the American Friars could not solve by themselves; thus two discreets, Servatius Altmicks and Kilian Schlösser, traveled to Saxonia. Apparently, they demanded that the mission be converted into an independent custody or province so that they would be able to continue their work in America without problems. This can be concluded from a letter which Janknecht wrote to the Minister General on the December 28, 1875, which reads: "*When the paters of the mission intended to separate from the province a year ago, I wrote to you with the same intention and it was only because we were in extreme danger of suppression at that time that I rejected the idea of separation in agreement with the definitorium.*"[107] As a result of this letter, on February 9 the paters from America received—together with a number of oral instructions—a document which more or less assured the independence of the commissariat, even if dependence on Saxonia still existed on paper. This measure was taken with the knowledge and permission of the General, with whom the American Friars were now allowed to correspond without consulting the Mother Province first. The only obligation of the Commissariat was to give a report four times a year.[108]

---

[107] Reinhold, Korrespondenz 60.

[108] Concerning the independence of the American mission Janknecht wrote to the General on December 28, 1875: „*Wegen der zu großen Distanz habe ich meinen Kommissar ad universitatem causam delegiert, so jedoch, daß er in wichtigen Fällen und besonders bei solchen, in denen auch der Provinzial nur im Einverständnis mit dem Definitorium handeln kann, immer das Einverständnis der Diskreten der Mission, die ich bei meiner Visitation in Amerika eingesetzt und deren Namen—wie alle meine Anordnungen— ich Ew. Paternität zur Approbation vorgelegt habe, einholen und erhalten muß. Wenn der Kommissar ihren Konsens erhalten hat, dann, so habe ich vor, will ich alles durch meine Autorität geschehen betrachten. Diesen Modus habe ich gewählt, damit man sich nicht über*

During the next year, the situation in Prussia deteriorated more and more until, as a result, the Franciscans were expelled from their convents due to the *Klostergesetz* of May 31, 1875. Whereas the older members of the province were accommodated in new convents in Holland and Belgium, Janknecht sent the majority of the younger Friars to the North American mission. In the above mentioned letter to the Minister General from December 28, Janknecht expressed his relief about the fact that the mission in North America had not yet become an independent province. *"If separation had taken place and our branch had been dissolved, we would have had to humbly ask for admission, whereas now, on the contrary, I can send people to America freely, as the well-being of the province and the well-being of each individual member requires and I will indeed send members there again next January. Thus, on the one hand the mission is independent of the province, but on the other, the Mother Province is able to intervene if necessary."*[109]

In 1875 alone 100 Friars and candidates of the Order joined the American Commissariat which, at that time, consisted of 124 members living in seven residences.[110] The following year, two smaller groups followed. The Commissary could not cope with such a large number of new Friars, so Klostermann, at Janknecht's direction, and after consulting his Discretorium, decided to take charge of several new residences. Several of these residences had to be built first, however. For this reason, many Friars could only be accommodated provisionally during the following years. Thus in the years between 1875 and 1879, ten new residences were established and four more were planned.

At the Provincial Chapter in February of 1876 in Püth, Holland the Definitorium decided unanimously to ask Janknecht to travel to

---

verspätete Antworten und Entscheidungen beklagen kann. Ferner könnte ich wohl kaum gegen eine einmütige Meinung des Kommissars und der Diskreten etwas tun." Reinhold, Korrespondenz 60.

[109] Reinhold, Korrespondenz 60. This remark reflects Janknecht's negative experiences in accommodating members of the Saxonia in Austrian convents. Thus, in his letter he wrote: *„daß die Errichtung der Mission in eine Provinz oder Kustodie vorläufig noch verschoben werde, bis die Situation in der Heimat sich geklärt habe."*

[110] Fleckenstein, Franziskaner 57, speaks of 117 members of the province including candidates who went to America in 1875. Janknecht himself in a letter to the General wrote on July 13, 1875 about 110 friars who had already arrived in America. Reinhold, Korrespondenz 55. Habig believes that 123 friars were sent into the American mission between 1875 and 1876; Habig, *Heralds* 113.

the North American mission as a visitator once again.[111] The radical changes there required close inspection and structured procedures. It is likely that this proposal had been initiated by Janknecht himself. A few weeks before he had written to the General: *"I love our American mission, I know it really well and I know how much good is being done for the salvation of the souls in its name. Nevertheless, I cannot conceal that it is in great danger. If your paternity wishes me to exercise jurisdiction in the American mission to a larger extent than I mentioned above, I am happy to do this and will be waiting for your orders. My only wish is that no other visitator from another province be appointed. Someone who is not well-acquainted with the conditions in a country in which the good and the bad reveals itself very clearly could easily be mistaken when evaluating the difficulties which arise concerning regular observance if he concentrates too much on practical work for saving the souls. Above all, it is important for the paters to be good Franciscans. When they give up this attitude, they will no longer be good missionaries."*[112] It is very probable that very few people within the province could live up to these expectations. For this reason, when Janknecht says in his letter to the General that he is ready to travel to America *in spite of the current political circumstances,*[113] this formula has to be considered a mere expression of humility. However, his journey was delayed several times by the impending war; Janknecht finally left for America with the last group of Friars on September 30, 1876.

After the Provincial arrived in America in October, he soon started his visitations. By November 15 he had visited the friaries in Cleveland, Indianapolis, St. Louis and Chicago and was staying in Jordan, Minnesota, for a while in order to finish his visits to the north *before the cold season was settled in.*[114] When he had finished his visitations, he traveled together with the Commissary, Klostermann, to several places which had been offered to the Franciscans in order to establish new friaries there. As a result, he called together the Discretorium for a meeting in St. Louis from January 13-17, 1877.[115]

[111] Reinhold, Korrespondenz 62.
[112] Reinhold, Korrespondenz 60.
[113] Reinhold, Korrespondenz 63.
[114] Reinhold, Korrespondenz 64.
[115] Janknecht had originally intended to gather this „Congregatio" at Christmas, if his visitation had not been delayed. On December 21 he wrote the General from

At this meeting a new Guardian was appointed for each of the houses. They were to be confirmed in office by the Definitorium of the Province in Holland. Furthermore, three new friaries were taken over and several regulations concerning the observance of the Rule, the Constitutions, and the Provincial Statutes were agreed upon.[116]

From the beginning, Janknecht had planned a longer stay as he wrote to the Minister General in 1876: *"For this reason, I have postponed my return until August. Thus I will be staying in America from September till April, so that our fellow brothers there cannot complain about my concluding the issue faster than acceptable."*[117] Nevertheless, his return was delayed again and again, so that he did not return to Europe until March of 1878 after a 16- month stay at the mission at the special request of his confreres in Holland and Belgium.

Several letters which Janknecht wrote during his time in America enable us to follow the course of his journey.[118] At the beginning of February he was staying with the Friars in Cleveland where he was dealing with the transfers that had been agreed upon at the meeting of the Discretorium in January. At the beginning of March, he went to Hoboken, New Jersey, in order to represent the interests of the friary

---

Memphis/Tennessee: „*Im Januar werde ich die Diskreten versammeln und die Wahl der Oberen unserer Mission vornehmen. Mit einer Ausnahme habe ich alle Konvente visitiert. Ich bin—Gott sie gedankt!—sehr zufrieden.*" Reinhold, Korrespondenz 64f.

[116] Janknecht had a great influence on these decisions. In a letter to the General dated February 22, 1877, he wrote: „*Die von mir vorgeschlagenen Oberen erhielten sämtlich alle Stimmen der Diskreten. Die Ordinationes, die ich für das Wohl der Mission notwendig und nützlich hielt, wurden einstimmig angenommen.*" Reinhold, Korrespondenz 65.

[117] Reinhold, Korrespondenz 63. In January 1877 the discreets met and urgently begged Janknecht to stay longer in America. Reinhold, Korrespondenz 65. In November 1877 Hyacinth Deimel wrote from the Saxonia to the Minister General: „*Er [Janknecht] hat auf Bitten der amerikanischen Mitbrüder seine Rückkehr verschoben, um den Stand der Mission besser kennenzulernen und alles Notwendige persönlich anzuordnen, zumal damals der Gesundheitszustand derKleriker nicht gerade der beste war. Dazu kommt noch der Erwerb von neuen Häusern, die er vorher alle selbst besichtigt. So arbeitet er auch unermüdlich an der Errichtung eines Gymnasiums im Konvent zu Cleveland für den Nachwuchs. All das kostet viel Geld, und so ist Rat und Hilfe des Provinzials nötig.*" Reinhold, Korrespondenz 66.

[118] Habig, *Heralds* 169 talks about 17 letters which Janknecht had written during this time and which are located in the archives of the Sacred Heart Province in St. Louis. However, according to the archivist there, the letters which Habig worked with cannot be found anymore.

in Mount Alverno. This residence, which had been founded shortly before, was to be consolidated with the house at Danville. However, this issue was not agreed upon during Janknecht's stay at Hoboken. There he caught a serious cold and suffered from a sore throat and fever for some time. In Indianapolis, Ferdinand Bergmeyer took over the position as Pastor and Superior of the residence. Janknecht stayed there for over a fortnight. At the request of Kilian Schlösser, he returned to Cleveland at the beginning of April, probably intending to leave for Chicago and Joliet from there. Afterwards, he spent a week at Hermann, Missouri. On April 18 he was staying at Teutopolis, and from there he traveled on to St. Louis. At that time, a German colony was being founded in Texas. The Franciscans were to be in charge of the pastoral care in this area. For this reason, Janknecht traveled to Texas together with P. Eugene Puers, but his mission turned out to be futile as the plan to place the Franciscans in charge was given up in the end. Thus Janknecht was back at Hermann on the May 17, 1877. On June 6, he was staying at the friary at Memphis. On August 30, he met Aloysius Lauer,[119] who was Custos of Thuringia at the time and later became Minister General. Together they traveled to Cincinnati to visit P. Dominic Droessler in the hospital. Janknecht went back to St. Louis via Hermann. On September 22 he seems to have stayed at Teutopolis for Klostermann's name-day celebration. On this occasion, plans to establish the new residence in Rhineland (Starkenburg), Missouri were also discussed. On November 1, 1877, Janknecht visited Jordan, Minnesota, and on February 4, 1878, he was in Memphis, Tennessee.

[119] Janknecht and Lauer had been together in the novitiate in the early 1850s and remained friends since then. In late 1855 Janknecht had also been Lauer's Provincial until the convents in Fulda and Salmünster were erected and an independent custody was established in December 1855. The two Franciscans continued a regular correspondence and met personally as often as possible. When Janknecht returned from Brazil critically ill in 1896, he telegraphed Lauer, but Lauer never saw his friend alive again. Then he wrote to Jeiler: *„Ich brauche Ihnen nicht zu sagen, welchen Eindruck dieser Todesfall auf mich gemacht hat, da Sie ja das Verhältnis kennen, in welchem ich zu dem Verstorbenen immer stand. Es tat mir sehr leid, daß ich ihn nicht mehr sprechen konnte; es war mir aber ein großer Trost, daß ich ihn wenigstens noch sehen und seinem Begräbnis beiwohnen konnte.“* Lauer wrote Janknecht's obituary since he was one of the editors of the *Acta Ordinis*. Enneking, Pater Aloys Lauer NF 35 (1980) 287 and 293. Janknecht's letters to Lauer from the years 1856-1858 are located in the archives of the Thuringian Province in Fulda under the signature I-B 05b.1 (118).

In 1879 the North American mission was organized as an independent Province. At the meeting of the Definitorium of Saxonia in Püth on September 17, 1878, the members agreed to ask the General to declare the Commissariat an independent Custody or Province. This request was granted by the General Definitorium on October 5, who decided to declare the mission an independent Province. Thus Janknecht was able to personally inform the Friars of the American mission of his decision on November 27 and leave it to each Friar to decide to return to the Mother Province or to be incorporated into the new entity. Only about thirty members of the Commissariat took advantage of the opportunity to return to Saxonia; the rest remained in the United States.[120] By decree of Pope Leo XIII, the North American mission was converted into an independent province named the Province of the Most Sacred Heart of Jesus on April 26, 1879. At that time, Sacred Heart Province consisted of 202 members, who lived in four convents and ten residences.[121] Janknecht himself chose the name of the new province at the request of the Minister General.[122]

For American Franciscans, Janknecht has always been remembered as the founder of the Province. For this reason, in 1958, the Provincial of the Sacred Heart Province, Pius Barth, suggested erecting a monument dedicated to Janknecht in his own Province in Germany. Subsequently, the Definitorium of the Saxonian Province decided to have a bronze relief bust made. Originally, this bust was to have been placed at Warendorf, but later it was decided to place it outside the college at Dorsten as this was close to Janknecht´s place of birth in Kirchhellen. On October 16 a ceremony was held at the Franciscan friary of Dorsten at which Provincial Pius Barth personally consecrated the bronze bust of Reverend P. Gregor Janknecht. The American daughter Province absorbed the $1,500.00 which it cost to have the bust created.[123]

---

[120] There are no exact numbers of how many friars returned to Europe. Kullmann, Willibald: *Die Sächsische Franziskanerprovinz. Ein tabellarischer Leitfaden ihrer Geschichte* (Düsseldorf, 1927), 29; Habig, *Heralds* 171f., Fleckenstein, Franziskaner 58.

[121] Kullmann, *Franziskanerprovinz* 29 and Fleckenstein, Franziskaner 58. Habig, *Heralds* 175 speaks about 12 residences since the two colleges in Teutopolis and Quincy count as separate residences. There are copies in Latin and German in the ASFP Werl.

[122] Reinhold, Korrespondenz 75f.

[123] Griesenbrock, Franziskaner 183. There are further letters in the ASFP Werl.

A letter from the Sacred Heart Province which was recently published in the official information service of the Saxonian Province shows how close the connections with the Mother Province remain to this day: *"We often speak about you with full gratitude—especially for what you have given us in 1858 and the following years: your Friars live on in our Province through your traditions and your character."*[124]

The Poor Clares in North America

Janknecht also took advantage of his stay in America to clarify the affairs of the Poor Clares. Before Janknecht left Europe, the minister general had already appealed to him to appoint a Franciscan confessor and a director for the Sisters.[125] Janknecht took this mission very seriously and thus dealt with the issue shortly after his arrival in America. *"Above all, I would like to inform you that I have arrived safely in New York after a rather turbulent crossing.[...] After a two- day stay with the brothers in Cleveland I went straight to the Poor Clares in Philadelphia in order to make inquiries there."*[126]

In this letter to the General, which Janknecht wrote from Jordan, Minnesota on November 15, he also explained the situation of the Poor Clares as he saw it. According to the information Janknecht had received, the Archbishop was no longer interested in establishing a residence of the Poor Clares and wanted the sisters to return to Rome as soon as possible. Janknecht, however, wanted to help them find an adequate building for their community. Moreover, he thought the foundation of the Poor Clares was possible in the United States even though the Americans *are practical people, who prefer monastic communities which lead an active life.*[127] Such an establishment, however, required a strict observance of the rules and a residence of the First Order situated close by. After he had suggested various possibilities for the successful foundation of a monastery of the Poor Clares in Minnesota without result, Janknecht finally obtained permission for a monastery of the Poor Clares in

---

[124] *Information-Dienst der Sächsischen Franziskanerprovinz vom Hl. Kreuz* 11/12 (November/Dezember 2002) 3.

[125] Reinhold, Korrespondenz 64-70.

[126] Reinhold, Korrespondenz 64.

[127] Reinhold, Korrespondenz 64.

Cleveland.[128] Consequently, the Poor Clares moved to Cleveland on August 9. Nevertheless, serious problems arose very soon and so the Sisters asked Janknecht to send for Sisters from Germany so that the Italian Sisters could return to Italy. The German sisters, who were living in exile in Holland at that time, agreed to send four Choir Sisters and one Lay Sister to America.[129] In the meantime, however, the Poor Clares in Cleveland had changed their minds and wanted to stay in America after all.[130] When the German Sisters arrived on December 15, 1877, there was an unfortunate turn of events concerning the foundation of the Poor Clares. Since the Italian Sisters were a minority, the stricter observance of the German Sisters applied. However, Janknecht granted a number of liberties to the Italian Sisters since he assumed that within a few months they would either leave or establish a new residence in South America. As early as January 1879, Janknecht was able to inform the General that the Poor Clares now had postulants. Moreover, he added that the major part of the $10,000.00 mortgage which the Franciscans had incurred to buy the house and the ground for the Sisters had already been paid off.[131]

4. Master of Novices and General Definitor 1861-1867

At the Provincial Chapter in 1861, Othmar Maasmann was elected the new Provincial on July 25. A month before, Maasmann had succeeded against Janknecht in the election as General Visitator of the Saxonian Province.[132] Since Janknecht was no longer Provincial of the Saxonian Province, he was no longer Guardian of

---

[128] When the Bishop of Cleveland asked Janknecht for a professor for the seminary, Janknecht pushed his demand for permission to found a residence for the Poor Clares. Reinhold, Korrespondenz 67

[129] These were Sisters from the convent in Dusseldorf. During the Kulturkampf they went first to Tongerlo near Lichtenvoorde in the Diocese of Utrecht. This place was not far from Harreveld. Thus, they were looked after by the Franciscans. After two years in Tongerlo the Sisters moved to Harreveld. See: Fleckenstein, Gisela: Frauen des Gebetes: Das Kloster der Klarissen in Düsseldorf 1859-1949. In: *Der eigene Blick. Frauen-Geschichte und -Kultur in Düsseldorf*. Ed. Ariane. Neuhaus-Koch, 2. Aufl. (Neuss, 1990), 93-106.

[130] Reinhold, Korrespondenz 67.

[131] Reinhold, Korrespondenz 68.

[132] ASFP Werl, Acta capitularia 1843-1888, 209f.

the friary in Dusseldorf either. However, he remained in Dusseldorf since he was appointed by the Chapter as Professor of Theology.[133] As former Provincial, Janknecht was still involved in the decisions of the Definitorium of the Province due to the Principle of Precedence. This is the reason why he was always part of the Province's leadership even at times when he was not Provincial or General Visitator.[134] Moreover, he held the title "Provinciae Pater" following the Chapter as the minutes of the Chapter show.[135]

Despite his young age—he was 32 years old—Janknecht was elected General Definitor of the Discalced and Recollect Franciscans at the General Chapter in Rome on June 14, 1862.[136] His efforts to re-organize the Saxonian Province, and especially his success in the North American mission, had deeply impressed the leadership of the Order. Thus they wanted to make use of this man's organizational talents for the whole Order. The fact that Janknecht was elected General Definitor by all members of the Chapter substantiates his good reputation within the Order.[137] All together, twelve General Definitors were elected in 1862. Only six of them had to stay permanently in Rome for the General's support. After 1869 all General Definitors had to be present in Rome.[138] Initially, Janknecht was not among the General Definitors who had to stay in Rome.[139] Consequently, he could fulfill his duties as Master of Novices in Warendorf between 1862 and 1866. Janknecht had officially received this task at the Midterm Chapter in Wiedenbrück in

---

[133] ASFP Werl, Acta capitularia 1843-1888, 245; Peters, Totenbuch II, 294.

[134] Fleckenstein, Franziskaner 37, 42.

[135] ASFP Werl, Acta capitularia 1843-1888, 245; also Fleckenstein, Franziskaner 36.

[136] *Capitulum Generale totius Ordinis Fratrum Minorum S.P.N. Francisci Romae in ve. Conventu S. Mariae de Aracoeli die 7 iunii 1862 celebratum.* (Romae, 1862), 79; *Acta Ordinis Minorum* 15 (1896) 60; Schmies / Rakemann, *Spuren* 483. Janknecht did not personally participate in this Chapter; see: *Capitulum Generale 1862*, 88.

[137] Besides Janknecht, there was only one other General Definitor who received 90 votes in this election. All the others received much less approval; *Capitulum Generale 1862*, 78f.

[138] *Capitulum Generale 1862*, 81; Holzapfel, *Handbuch* 434.

[139] Compare the General Definitors in *Capitulum Generale 1862*, 81. Obviously it was planned that the two groups of Definitors should change every two years. Perhaps the difficult personnel situation in Saxonia and the need for him as Master of Novices allowed Janknecht to stay in Saxonia until 1866 before he moved to Rome.

October 1862. The previous Master of Novices, Mathias Hiltermann, had been called to North America to serve as Provincial Commissioner.[140] Janknecht served in this position until he had to move to Rome as Definitor in 1866.[141] During his stay in Rome, Janknecht became seriously ill. During a subsequent journey to Egypt and Palestine at the beginning of 1867 a Doctor Bellanti diagnosed nervous gastritis caused by the unfamiliar dining and living habits in Italy. In this Italian medical certificate Bellanti confirms that Janknecht could no longer stay in Italy without putting his health at serious risk.[142] Because of this Janknecht repeatedly asked the General to release him from the obligation of residence in Rome. However, the General did not accede to his request. Nevertheless, Janknecht did not return to Rome after his pilgrimage but went home to Saxonia. He later explained this decision as the consequence of his appointment as General Visitator to his own Province in February 1867.[143] At the end of this visitation Janknecht was elected Provincial Minister at the Provincial Chapter in July 1867. This election notwithstanding, he remained a General Definitor. In order for him to fulfill both roles at the same time and because of his poor health, the Minister General, Raphael Lippi of Ponticulo, fully released him from his duty of being present in Rome.[144] It can

---

[140] ASFP Werl, Acta capitularia 1843-1888, 258; Beiträge zur Geschichte des Noviziates 161f. Peters, *Totenbuch* II, 263. Probably Janknecht took over the leadership of the novitiate earlier since Mathias Hiltermann had left for America already on May 15, 1862 (Habig, *Heralds* 80).

[141] AG OFM Rom, SK 499 fol. 251r+v (Alexandrien, 16. Januar 1867). This medical certificate mentions a seven-month stay in Rome before Janknecht's trip to Egypt and Palestine. Consequently, Janknecht must have left for Rome in May or June of 1866. This assumption is confirmed by the fact that there are no letters from Janknecht to the General between April of 1866 and his pilgrimage (see AG OFM Rom, SK 499). Janknecht usually wrote regularly to Rome. This was not necessary when he was there himself at this time. Consequently, Janknecht headed the Novitiate only until 1866 and not until 1867 as Peters, *Totenbuch* II, 263 mentions. Since there was no Provincial Chapter in 1866, the new Master of Novices, Silvester Winkes, was not appointed before the Chapter in 1867.

[142] AG OFM Rom, SK 499 fol. 251r+v (Alexandrien, 16. Januar 1867).

[143] AG OFM Rom, SK 499, fol. 264r+v (Wiedenbrück, 25. April 1867).

[144] ASFP Werl, Personalakte P. Gregor Janknecht, Schreiben des Generalministers vom 7. September 1867; see also ASFP Werl, Rundschreiben, Gregor Janknecht 1867-1879 (Warendorf, 15. Oktober 1867). Loddenkötter, P. Gregor 223.

only be approximated how long Janknecht served as General Definitor.[145] As far as I can determine, Janknecht's circular letter to Saxonia dated February 16, 1869, is the last document that he signed as General Definitor.[146] Evidently, then, his term lasted for almost seven years. Since the Minister General was elected at the Chapter in 1862 for twelve years—instead of six years as was done previously—it is likely that the General Definitors held their office for the same length of time. However, General Raphael Lippi of Ponticulo officially resigned from his office on April 23, 1869.[147] Perhaps the General Definitors were also released from their office at the same time. This is indicated by the fact that Janknecht did not refer to his title as General Definitor in a letter of May 16, 1869 to the new Minister General. He signed it as Minister Provincial.[148] It is possible that he was no longer General Definitor by then. One of Janknecht's letters to the commissioner in the North American mission, Kilian Schlösser, was written from Rome on March 13, 1869. Obviously, Janknecht was in Rome at this time in order to be present at the deliberations about a successor for the General. It is not clear whether new General Definitors were elected at that occasion or if Janknecht resigned from his office because of his many duties in the Province. However, Janknecht was the only member of the Saxonian Province who served in the leadership of the Order during the entire 19th century.[149]

As previously mentioned, Janknecht was General Visitator to the Saxonian Province in the years 1864[150] and 1867.[151] A General Visitation takes place before every Provincial Chapter. Generally, it should be carried out by a Friar external to the Province who is appointed after consultation with the General Definitorium and the

---

[145] The literature gives different dates. Loddenkötter, P. Gregor 223 comes closest. Mathes, *Tugendsterne* 300, Kullmann, P. Gregor 55 and Griesenbrock, *500 Jahre*, 174 are wrong.

[146] ASFP Werl, Rundschreiben, Gregor Janknecht 1867-1879 (St. Apollinarisberg, 16. Februar 1869).

[147] Holzapfel, *Handbuch* 372, 692.

[148] AG OFM Rom, SK 499 fol. 286r+v (Warendorf, 16. Mai 1867).

[149] Compare the list of General Definitors in Peters, *Totenbuch* II, 231.

[150] Peters, *Totenbuch* II, 232; ASFP Werl, Acta capitularia 1843-1888, 269.

[151] Peters, *Totenbuch* II, 232; ASFP Werl, Acta capitularia 1843-1888, 319. See also AG OFM Rom, SK 499 fol. 264 (Alexandrien, 25. April 1867).

Minister General.[152] An important component of a visitation is a personal talk with each member of the Province being visited. Thus, it is important that the Visitator speak the local language. That is how every Friar would be able to speak anonymously about any deplorable state of affairs in the Province. This also helped the Visitator to evaluate the observance of the rule and statutes. The General received a report of the visitation. The visitation concluded with the Provincial Chapter which was presided over by the Visitator. This is the reason why former Provincials and Definitors were usually appointed as Visitators.[153] Although the two friaries of the Thuringian Custody had become independent in December of 1855 after two years in the Saxonian Province, they were visited by the same Visitator but dealt with separately. Consequently, Janknecht also visited the Thuringian Custody in 1864 and 1867.[154] On June 7, 1864, Janknecht wrote a short report to the General about his visitation.[155]

During the 1860s Janknecht was in close contact with Franziska Schervier, the foundress of the Poor Sisters of St. Francis in Aachen.[156] While she was trying to establish a Franciscan convent in Aachen, Schervier contacted Janknecht, who was Provincial at that time. Numerous letters between Schervier and Janknecht demonstrate that she often asked him for advice and counted on his support.[157] Janknecht's connection with the women Franciscans was so

[152] This principle was not observed in Saxonia in the 1860s. The third visitation of the decade was carried out by Othmar Maasmann. There had been several other visitations from members of the Province during the early years of the 19th century (Peters, *Totenbuch* II, 232). This circumstance can be explained by the difficult condition in which the Order was at that time. However, it is not clear why the Order acted the same way during the 1860s. See also: Reinhold, Alkantarinenbewegung 236.

[153] Fleckenstein, Franziskaner 160-162.

[154] In 1858 P. Natalis Neuteleers from the Belgian St. Joseph Province had visitated the Saxonia Province and the Thuringian Custody. Enneking, Pater Aloys Lauer *NF* 35 (1980) 459, 463; *NF* 36 (1981) 112.

[155] AG OFM Rom, SK 499 fol. 223r+v (Warendorf, 7. Juni 1864).

[156] See: Lang, Justin: „Schervier, Franziska." In: *Lexikon für Theologie und Kirche.* Bd. 9. 9Freiburg/Br. U.a., 20000, Sp. 132. More detailed in Troxler, Walter: „Schervier, Franziska." In: *Biographisch-Bibliographisches Lexikon.* Bd. 9. (Herzberg, 1995), Sp. 170f. Also in: Jeiler, *Mutter.*

[157] Unfortunately, only Schervier's letters to Janknecht have been preserved. They are in the Provincial Archives: ASFP Werl, Nachlaß Ignatius Jeiler Nr. 455. There are also copies in the Mother House of the Poor Sisters of St. Francis in Aachen. See:

close that he even visited their residences in America during his trips in 1860 and 1877.[158]

5. Provincial from 1867 till 1879

The Provincial Chapter in Wiedenbrück on July 9, 1867 overwhelmingly elected Janknecht as Provincial again.[159] During his term he resided in the friary in Warendorf[160] where he had already spent the previous years except for his time in Rome and America. The main stress of his first term was on the American mission and his second visitation there. Since this was already mentioned in Chapter 3, it will not be repeated here.

Janknecht was reelected by a large majority at the next Provincial Chapter in Paderborn on September 8, 1870.[161] The Minister General Bernardino dal Vago da Portugruaro himself was the chair of the Chapter. He had previously conducted the visitation of the Saxonian Province.[162] On the occasion of the visitation, Leo Rinklage wrote the General on July 18, 1870—still before Janknecht's reelection—complaining that the overseers of the Province never change. Bernardino dal Vago personally referred to Janknecht's and Maasmann's great achievements for the Province and called Leo a jealous man of evil character.[163] This reaction demonstrates Janknecht's and Maasmann's

---

Nickel, Ralf (Bearb.): *Nachlaß P. Dr. Ignatius Jeiler OFM (1823-1904) in the archives in Werl, Westfalia.* Janknecht had given his letters from Schervier to Jeiler in 1887 for his research about Franziska Schervier. ASFP Werl, Nachlaß Ignatius Jeiler Nr. 73 (St. Apollinarisberg, 20. März 1887) as well as Nickel, Nachlaß 28. Janknecht's letters to Schervier have not been preserved. I know of only one letter from January 14, 1864: ASFP Werl, Nachlaß Ignatius Jeiler Nr. 455, also in: ASFP Werl, Personalakte P. Gregor Janknecht.

[158] Habig, *Heralds* 58; Reinhold, Korrespondenz 66.

[159] Janknecht received 16 votes in the last ballot, while Maasmann received only one. See: Acta capitularia 1843-1888, 323, 326, 335.

[160] Acta capitularia 1843-1888, 335; also in the documents from the Chapter which were sent to the General: AG OFM Rom, SK 499 fol. 269r, 9. Juli 1867.

[161] Janknecht received 15 votes and Maasmann one; Acta capitularia 1843-1888, 363.

[162] Schmies / Rakemann, *Spuren* 487.

[163] ASFP Werl, Karteikarten Julius Reinhold (18. Juli 1870). A majority of Saxonia's correspondence between the years 1870 and 1879 is documented on these index cards—specially Janknecht's. Moreover, they contain some information about

high standing before the General. During his stay in the Province he developed a friendship with them and he even invited them both to his consecration as Archbishop in 1892.[164]

The General's visitation led to a turn towards Roman customs in Saxonia.[165] Janknecht was always intent on Rome's wishes and ideas.[166] This may be the result of his strong connection with Rome during his term as General Definitor. Besides that, Janknecht subscribed to the ultramontanist attitude which was widespread at that time and which dominated the First Vatican Council in 1869-1870.[167] Janknecht was skeptical towards Modernism and adhered to the conditions and traditions of the past. His ultramontanist attitude appears quite clearly in a letter to the General of November 1871 in which he voiced his suspicion against the Altkatholiken.[168]

Another example of Janknecht's ultramontanist attitude is his proceeding against the scientific work of his confrere Bernhard Döbbing. Janknecht as well as Maasmann and Jeiler opposed the publication of Döbbing's work since it did not always correspond with the doctrines

---

the history of the Province in the first half of the 19th century. Reinhold probably produced these cards during the research for his essay Reinhold, Korrespondenz, where most of his notes were used. Leo Rinklage was born on December 10, 1833; entered the novitiate on October 12, 1854, and was ordained a priest on December 19, 1859. Later, he went to the North American mission, where he taught at the college in Teutopolis from 1872 till 1873. On October 17, 1873 he died from the Yellow Fever; Peters, *Totenbuch* I, 308 and Peters; *Totenbuch* II, 174 as well as AG OFM Rom, C40 (Historia Provinciae S. Crucis) fol. 152v. For Janknecht's opinion on this reproach see Reinhold, Korrespondenz 79.

[164] Kullmann, P. Gregor 55; Conlan, Patrick: *St. Isidore's College Rome*, (Rome, 1982), 182.

[165] Reinhold, Korrespondenz 47.

[166] Kullmann, P. Gregor 105. Janknecht's loyalty towards Rome was also mentioned in a poem after his death: „Fünfmal stand er an dem Steuerruder / Schaut nach Romas Leuchtturm unverwandt." Schulte, Konrad, Am Grabe von P. Gregor Janknecht O.S.F. Paderborn 1. März 1896. In: *Antoniusbote* 2 (1895/1896) 346; copied in Kullmann, P. Gregor 58 and Büning; Pater Gregor Janknecht 334. He visited Rome eight times. „Seit dem 23. November vorigen Jahres bin ich zum 8. Male in Rom." ASFP Werl, Personalakte P. Gregor Janknecht, Postkarte mit Brief an Andreas Hartmann (Paderborn) (Rom, 10. Januar 1894).

[167] About Ultramontanism: Lill, Rudolf: Der Ultramontanismus. Die Ausrichtung der gesamten Kirche auf den Papst. In: Weitlauff, Manfred (Ed.): *Kirche im 19. Jahrhundert* (Regensburg, 1998), 76-94, 222.

[168] Reinhold, Korrespondenz 48.

espoused by the Province.[169] Rome, as well as Janknecht and Maasmann as the Saxonian Province's leading authorities, did not accept any independent theology besides the scholastic method.[170] Scholasticism, they believed, was the only approach acceptable for coping with modern sciences. Everything else threatened to open the door to modernism and thus endanger the restoration of the church.[171]

In general, Janknecht had a positive attitude towards science, and regarded it as extremely important; he tried to promote it wherever possible. This attitude was already clear in his first circular letter to the Province.[172] Since the Minister General Bernardino dal Vago revived philosophical and theological studies in the Order during his two-year term, Janknecht also had sufficient opportunity to promote the sciences. He did so by supplying personnel and material support for the critical edition of the *opera omnia* of Bonaventure, which was initiated by the General.[173] Janknecht regularly sent Friars for this project, which was based in Quaracchi from 1877 on.[174] Italian and Saxonian Friars were the main editors of the works of Bonaventure.

Janknecht attributed the fortunate outcome of the German-French War to the Sacred Heart of Jesus. He wrote in a letter to the General on March 10, 1871: "*We owe it to the SS. Heart of Jesus, whose special protection we have received.*"[175] As usual Janknecht indulged in devotion to the Sacred Heart, for which he had a special fondness.[176] It was a typical expression of popular piety during the 19th cen-

---

[169] Fleckenstein, Franziskaner 271. See also Reinhold, Übersicht 236f.

[170] Fleckenstein, Franziskaner 271.

[171] Nipperdey describes that as follows: „Es kam nicht auf gelehrte, sondern auf fromme und gehorsame Priester an." „Zur Verkündigung der Kirche gehört schließlich die scharfe Abgrenzung gegen die Welt, die moderne, die feindliche Welt." Nipperdey, Thomas: *Religion im Umbruch. Deutschland 1870-1918.* (München, 1988), 14, 22.

[172] ASFP Werl, Rundschreiben, Gregor Janknecht 1855-1861 (Wiedenbrück, 29. September 1855).

[173] Fleckenstein, Franziskaner 244-251.

[174] Reinhold, Korrespondenz 51, 70f., 80.

[175] Quoted after ASFP Werl, Karteikarten Julius Reinhold (23. März 1871). The original is in AG OFM Rom, SK 499 fol. 336r+v.

[176] *Acta Ordinis Minorum* 15 (1896) 60; Kullmann, P. Gregor 104f.; Loddenkötter, P. Gregor 213. Also see Busch, Norbert: *Katholische Frömmigkeit und Moderne. Die Sozial- und Mentalitätsgeschichte des Herz-Jesu-Kultes in Deutschland zwischen dem Kulturkampf und dem Ersten Weltkrieg* (Gütersloh, 1997) (Religiöse Kulturen der Moderne, 6).

tury.[177] Devotion to the Sacred Heart developed in the bishoprics of Munster and Paderborn during the 1840s. It was spread especially by the mendicant orders. A special advocate of devotion to the Sacred Heart was the Bishop of Paderborn, Konrad Martin, with whom Janknecht was in close contact.[178] Janknecht himself was also an early supporter of this devotion. He referred to it in his first circular letter as Provincial dated September 29, 1855: *"Where will we take our necessary virtues from? Where from if not from the divine heart of our adorable Savior?"*[179] There is almost no letter from Janknecht in which he did not refer to the assistance of the heart of Jesus. Such references did not depend on the recipient of the letter or the official or personal character of the letter.[180] His actions were also influenced by this devotion. In the face of the *Kulturkampf* he put the entire Saxonian Province under the protection of the Sacred Heart on November 13, 1873.[181] Finally, Janknecht chose the title Sacred Heart for the Daughter Province in the US. The intensification of the devotion during the *Kulturkampf* corresponded with the general developments in Germany. The troubling conflicts between the State and the Church had "a traumatic effect and ignited apocalyptic fears." The Sacred Heart was "a symbol of identification for the contemporary suffering experienced by the Catholics." Thus the devotion rose to "one of the most practiced forms of popular Catholic religiosity."[182]

Perhaps it was this unconditional trust in the power of the Sacred Heart as well as God's Mother which gave Janknecht the strength to

[177] Blackbourn, David: *Volksfrömmigkeit und Fortschrittsglaube im Kulturkampf.* (Stuttgart, 1988) (Institut für Europäische Geschichte Mainz, Vorträge 81), 12.

[178] Busch, *Katholische Frömmigkeit* 69-71; Busch, Norbert: Fromme Westfalen. Zur Sozial- und Mentalitätsgeschichte des Herz-Jesu-Kultes in Deutschland zwischen dem Kulturkampf und dem Ersten Weltkrieg. In: *Westfälische Zeitschrift* 144 (1994) 329-350, here 331-335.

[179] ASFP Werl, Rundschreiben, Gregor Janknecht 1855-1861 (Wiedenbrück, 29. September 1855).

[180] Examples are Janknecht's letters to Döbbing; ASFP Werl, Nachlaß Bernhard Döbbing, Janknecht an Döbbing.

[181] ASFP Werl, Rundschreiben, Gregor Janknecht 1855-1861 (Münster, 14. Mai 1875) as well as Fleckenstein, Franziskaner 61, 137.

[182] Busch, Norbert: Frömmigkeit als Faktor des katholischen Milieus. Der Kult zum Herzen Jesu. In: Blaschke, Olaf / Kuhlemann, Frank-Michael (Ed.): *Religion im Kaiserreich* (Gütersloh, 1996) (Religiöse Kulturen der Moderne, 2) 136-165, here 141, 152, 154.

support other spiritual communities even in difficult times. Quite by accident, Janknecht met with the clergyman Arnold Janssen, the founder of Divine Word Missionaries, in the Munster Friary in the beginning of the year 1875. During their talk, Janknecht found out that Janssen needed a large sum of money for the establishment of a new mission house. Since Janknecht was very interested in the missions, he regarded the project worthy of his support. He had a chance to lend assistance the following month. Through Janknecht's arrangement, Janssen received 9,000 Marks which were the basis for the mission house in Steyl. Later Janknecht participated in the education of missionaries in Steyl and corresponded with Arnold Janssen occasionally.[183]

5.1 Provincial During the First Phase of the Kulturkampf

The so-called Prussian *Kulturkampf* under Bismarck exposed the Saxonian Province of the Holy Cross to new difficulties. After the Franciscans had slowly recovered from the effects of Secularization, the Province was faced with heavy repressive measures. During the first years of this conflict between the State and the Catholic Church, the leadership of the Province was in Janknecht's hands. Thanks to his "creative and innovative"[184] leadership, the Province was strengthened in personnel and conviction after the conflict was over—even though this had not been the State's intention.

The *Kulturkampf* started with the closing of the Catholic Department in the Prussian Ministry of the Arts on July 8, 1871.[185] The Saxonian Province felt the first impact of the *Kulturkampf* in December 1872 when the local school inspection was withdrawn

---

[183] Alt, Josef: *Arnold Janssen. Lebensweg und Lebenswerk des Steyler Ordensgründers.* (Nettetal, 1999) (Studia Instituti Missiologici Societatis Verbi Divini, 70) 75f.; ASFP Werl, Nachlaß Bernhard Döbbing, Janknecht an Döbbing (Harreveld, 5. März 1886).

[184] Fleckenstein, Franziskaner 320.

[185] The reasons for and effects of the Kulturkampf cannot be explained in detail in this place. For a more detailed description see: Morsey, Rudolf: Der Kulturkampf. Bismarcks Präventivkrieg gegen das Zentrum und die katholische Kirche. In. Manfred Weitlauff (Ed.): *Kirche im 19. Jahrhundert.* (Regensburg, 1998), 163-185, here 167. The texts of the laws are in: Huber, Ernst Rudolf / Huber, Wolfgang: *Staat und Kirche im 19. und 20. Jahrhundert. Dokumente zur Geschichte des deutschen Staatskirchenrechts. Vol. 2: Staat und Kirche im Zeitalter des Hochkonstitutionalismus und des Kulturkampfes 1848-1890.* (Berlin, 1976), especially 522-690.

from P. Basilius Pfannenschmid from Hardenberg-Neviges after the *Schulaufsichtsgesetz* dated March 11, 1872.[186] A month before, Janknecht had mentioned the expected measures against the Franciscans in a letter to the General. A few weeks before, the government had been rather obliging when it excluded clerics from military service. However, Janknecht's suspicion became clear when he asked for Papal permission to sell the convents with all movable goods if necessary.[187] From the very beginning Janknecht was very cautious and carefully observed political developments. He prepared to react quickly if necessary. His letters to the General show that initially he had hoped that the Province might remain unmolested. After the May Laws from 1873, however, it was certain that "*all bishops, priests and members of religious orders would be persecuted.*"[188] Janknecht tried to draw as little attention to the Province as possible. Consequently, he refused to accept the "beautiful friary in Bonn," which the Jesuits had to abandon after their Order had been expelled from Prussia by the *Jesuitengesetz*.[189] Janknecht was also very cautious with popular missions.[190] Janknecht changed his tactics after the May Laws were extended to members of religious Orders. Perhaps he thought that conflict was unavoidable. Nevertheless, on requests from Munster and Cologne he permitted a Franciscan to preach in the Cathedrals for the time of fasting, even though he feared a conflict with the government.[191]

In the course of the following months Saxonia started to feel the *Kulturkampf*. On September 12, 1874, Janknecht reported that P. Thomas Klarholz was forbidden to take the pastoral care of Remagen so that Janknecht himself had to help out with the confessions.[192]

[186] Fleckenstein, Franziskaner 47.

[187] Reinhold, Korrespondenz 48 (Warendorf, 11. November 1872). The Papal Dispensation was later permitted by the General Procurator. Janknecht then wrote to dal Vago: „Ich werde aber von dieser Fakultät nur im äußersten Notfall Gebrauch machen." Reinhold, Korrespondenz 48 (Warendorf, 13. Januar 1873).

[188] Reinhold, Korrespondenz 48f. (Warendorf, 16. Mai 1873).

[189] Reinhold, Korrespondenz 49 (Warendorf, 13. Januar 1873).

[190] Gatz, Erwin: *Rheinische Volksmission im 19. Jahrhundert dargestellt am Beispiel des Erzbistums Köln.* (Düsseldorf, 1963) (Studien zur Kölner Kirchegeschichte, 7), here 175.

[191] Reinhold, Korrespondenz 49 (Warendorf, 21. Januar 1874).

[192] Klarhalz's prohibition was later withdrawn; Reinhold, Korrespondenz 50 (Remagen, 12. September 1874). Besides that, Janknecht regularly helped out in Remagen for the confessions at Easter and Christmas. Erinnerungen an P. Gregorius

Soon afterwards the Franciscans in Hardenberg, Düsseldorf and Remagen were prohibited from collecting alms.[193] The friaries in Paderborn, Werl and Rietberg were searched.[194] In the spring of 1875 nine priests of the Province had to appear in court because of their pastoral work. The accused did not appear since that would have meant acceptance of the laws. Two of the priests were sentenced to two days of imprisonment. The fate of the seven other accused was not mentioned by Janknecht again.[195]

All these incidents motivated Janknecht to prepare the Province for the possible expulsion. He tried to find housing in the Bohemian Province.[196] Soon afterwards Janknecht found provisional accommodations in Holland close to the border.[197] He tried to find more houses along the border, since the expulsion of the Orders who were not active in the care of the sick seemed to be unavoidable. On May 6, 1875, he wrote to the Minister General: "*The majority of our Province will go to America. Besides that I have established three or four houses along the Prussian border.*"[198] The establishment of the new houses as well as the Friars' journey to America created enormous expenses for the Province. Janknecht asked the General for a dispensation to accept money in order to pay the bills. Since time was short, Janknecht asked the General to "*telegraph dispense accordée.*"[199] Besides that he asked for permission for some members of the Province to wear secular clothes. They had to stay in the old friaries and look after them. The sale of the convents was forbidden by the government, so that the Franciscans rented them out to benefactors of the Order for 10-15 years. The General permitted all these dispensations.[200]

Janknecht. In: *Vita Franciscana. Anregungen und Nachrichten aus der Provinz von der Unbefleckten Empfängnis in Südbrasilien 3* (1926) 39-45, here 41. Also in Kullmann, P. Gregor 106.

[193] Reinhold, Korrespondenz 50f. (Warendorf, 14. November 1874); Fleckenstein, Franziskaner 47.

[194] Reinhold, Korrespondenz 50f. (Warendorf, 14. November 1874).

[195] Reinhold, Korrespondenz 52 (Warendorf, 23. März 1875 / Warendorf, 31. März 1875 / Warendorf, 12. April 1875).

[196] Reinhold, Korrespondenz 52 (Warendorf, 12. April 1875).

[197] Reinhold, Korrespondenz 53 (Warendorf, 3. Mai 1875).

[198] Reinhold, Korrespondenz 53 (Warendorf, 6. Mai 1875).

[199] Reinhold, Korrespondenz 53 (Warendorf, 6. Mai 1875).

[200] Reinhold, Korrespondenz 54 (Münster, 3. Juni 1875).

One of Janknecht's main concerns was to keep the Friars informed about the current situation of the Province. On the one hand he tried to calm the Friars. On the other hand he hoped to prevent some of them from leaving the Order because of the difficult conditions. This was the reason for his circular letter dated May 14, 1875, in which he informed the Friars about the future of the Province. Furthermore, he insisted upon the observance of the Rule. He dedicated one section to the older Friars and ensured them that they would always be looked after.[201] Obviously, this circular letter was written at the right time and struck the right note, which demonstrates Janknecht's strength as a leader and his organizational talent. The reactions from the Province followed soon afterwards: "*All members of the Province are aroused enthusiastically; even the last aspirant is longing for obedience and would rather leave his homeland and parents than to be unfaithful to his profession.*"[202]

The *Klostergesetz* of May 31 *concerning all spiritual Orders and congregations of the Catholic Church* was announced on June 3, 1875. Thus, the fear of the Franciscans being expelled from Prussia had now come true. Janknecht acted without hesitation. He turned to the Austrian Emperor Franz Josef I and asked permission for the Friars to settle in the Bohemian Province. Janknecht visited Vienna and Prague twice during the following months, in order to negotiate with the Provincial and to speak to the Emperor personally.[203] However, his efforts were in vain. The Bohemian Province was suspicious of Janknecht's plea. Perhaps the Reform Province feared an estrangement of its Friars because of the presence of the Saxonian Recollect Province. The Emperor generally supported Janknecht's request. However, the request had to come from the office of the Bishop. Finally, the conditions of the Austrian Department of Education and Cultural Affairs were another obstacle. Thus, Janknecht's attempt to settle the Saxonian Franciscans in a German-speaking Province failed.[204]

---

[201] ASFP Werl, Rundschreiben, Gregor Janknecht 1855-1861 (Münster, 14. Mai 1875). There is a summary of the circular letter in Reinhold, Korrespondenz 54f.

[202] Reinhold, Korrespondenz 55 (Münster, 13. Juli 1875).

[203] Janknecht was there from the middle of July until the beginning of August and then again from the middle of September until the beginning of November. Fleckenstein, Franziskaner 49, Anm. 30 as well as Reinhold, Korrespondenz 56-58 (Wien, 20. Juli 1875 / Wien, 23. September 1875).

[204] Fleckenstein, Franziskaner 56f.

In the meantime, the Saxonians had to vacate several friaries. Janknecht realized that: "*The Prussian Government took stronger action against us than against the Jesuits. They had half a year to leave the country.*"[205] Janknecht did not return to Germany when he came back from Austria, but went straight into exile in Harreveld, Holland.[206] Even though Janknecht did not find accommodations in Austria, the letter to the General after his return sounded rather optimistic. The situation was not as bad as anticipated. The alms from German benefactors still reached the Saxonian Franciscans in sufficient amounts. And even new candidates and novices joined the Order. Consequently, a new novitiate could be opened in Harreveld in October 1875.[207] Janknecht's main goal was to re-establish the regular routine of the Order. The observance of the Rule and the statutes was paramount. This is the reason why he refused to allow the Friars in Dusseldorf to leave the Order so that they might continue the pastoral care of the local church as secular priests.[208] By December 1875, life in the Belgian and Dutch Friaries had returned to normal so that he could revoke the dispensations concerning the acceptance of money and the wearing of secular clothes. He expected the Friars to live a life in accordance with the Rule. He had bought new friaries for the members of his Province because strict observance in Saxonia was important to him. In the years after Secularization he had devoted much energy to promoting the former observance. He did not want to endanger his success by accommodating the Friars in different Provinces. "*Otherwise it would be difficult to re-establish the same observance with all of its many dif-*

---

[205] Reinhold, Korrespondenz 58 (Wien, 23. September 1875).

[206] Reinhold, Korrespondenz 58 (Harreveld, 11. November 1875). One of the reasons for his trip to Austria was to avoid public examinations. Reinhold, Korrespodenz, 55 (Bamberg, 9. Juli 1875).

[207] Reinhold, Korrespondenz 58 (Harreveld, 11. November 1875). The first investment in Harreveld took place on November 29, 1875. Officially, Harreveld became novitiate at the Provincial Chapter in Püth in February of 1876. Fleckenstein, Franziskaner 62.

[208] Reinhold, Korrespondenz 58 (Harreveld, 11. November 1875). Janknecht made only one exception in Hardenberg-Neviges in June 1875. He allowed the three Friars there to leave the Order so that they could secure the pastoral care of the parish and the place of pilgrimage. However, he tried not to arouse too much public interest. See: Fleckenstein, Franziskaner 62.

ferent elements after the current crisis is over."[209] At the end of 1875 the Saxonian Province had six friaries in Holland and Belgium at its disposal—enough for the accommodation of the Friars.[210] Thus, the most important measures for a regular life in exile had been finished: "*Now, everything is well arranged.*"[211]

Now, the Provincial Chapter could finally take place in Püth in February 1876 after it had been postponed several times. There the new Guardians of the new friaries were elected. Besides that the Chapter passed several regulations which were important for their life in exile, *i.e.* the careful regulation of trips to Prussia. These were indispensable in order to collect alms. The Franciscans still depended on money from Prussian friends. Since the Dutch and Belgian population consisted mainly of poor Protestant farmers, there was little possibility for termination of such trips. The fact that the majority of Catholic Orders expelled from Prussia had settled in this area, made the situation even worse. Nevertheless, the condition of the Province seemed stable enough so that Janknecht could be sent to conduct a visitation of the American Mission. The journey started the same year and lasted for several months.[212]

Janknecht continued the establishment of the Franciscans in their exile during the following years. In the spring of 1876 he purchased two more houses for the Province. One was in Verviers, Belgium, where the Franciscans took over the spiritual care of the Poor Sisters of St. Francis from Aachen. The other was in Watersleyde, Holland, where the Seraphic College from St. Annaberg in Silesia was reopened.

After Janknecht's return from America in March 1878, he probably celebrated his Silver (25th) Jubilee as a priest, which had taken place during his trip. On this occasion the Friars from Warendorf, with whom he had moved to Harreveld, gave him a silver Mass Cup with the inscription: "*A.R.P. Prov. Gregorio Janknecht in memoriam Jubilaei XXV annorum Conventus Warendorpiensis.*"[213] After that he visited the Friaries in Holland and Belgium and was very content with

---

[209] Reinhold, Korrespoindenz (Harreveld, 11. Dezember 1875).

[210] There were five Dutch friaries in Beezel, Harreveld, Brunsum, Püth and Bleyerheide and one Belgian residence in Moresnet; Fleckenstein, Franziskaner 58.

[211] Reinhold, Korrespondenz 55 (Harreveld, 28. Dezember 1875).

[212] See Chapter 3.

[213] Today, the Cup is in the friary in Osnabruck.

their condition. Shortly afterwards the American Mission was separated from the Mother Province. Both parts of the Province were able "*to exist and prosper separately.*"[214] This decision symbolized a significant change in the thinking of the leadership of the Province. Initially, the exile outside of Prussia was regarded as a provisional situation. However, by this time, the residences in Holland and Belgium were gradually regarded as a permanent solution. However, the Friars did not fully give up their hope of returning to Prussia.[215] This attitude becomes clear in several of Janknecht's letters to the General. At the beginning of the *Kulturkampf* he assumed that the conflict would not last long. His letter dated December 28, 1875, sounds rather pessimistic, however. He expresses his hope to re-purchase the Prussian friaries one day.[216] During the following years there were extensive construction projects[217] at the Dutch and Belgian friaries. This clearly indicates the long-term planning of the Provincial leadership. At the end of the 1870s Janknecht's attitude about the return to Prussia had become more optimistic. One reason may have been the election of the Parliament in 1878 which had a positive result for the Catholics.[218] In his next letter to the General, Janknecht had no doubt that the Province could return to its former friaries before long.[219] Shortly afterwards, Janknecht stepped down form his office of Provincial after twelve consecutive years.

5.2 *Retirement vs. Duty*

When Janknecht had been elected Provincial in 1870, a nine-year term began. Together with the three previous years, he served as Provincial for twelve years. In 1870 this development could not have been foreseen. At this time there were no indications that his term would last longer than the usual three years. However, the

---

[214] Reinhold, Korrespondenz 72 (Püth, 17. September 1878).

[215] Fleckenstein, Franziskaner 63.

[216] Reinhold, Korrespondenz 60 (Harreveld, 28. Dezember 1875).

[217] The friaries in Harreveld, Bleyerheide and Moresnet were new buildings. Müllejans, Rita: *Klöster im Kulturkampf. Die Ansiedlung katholischer Orden und Kongregationen aus dem Rheinland undihre Klosterneubauten im belgisch-niederländischen Grenzraum infolge des preußischen Kulturkampfs.* (Aachen, 1992) (Veröffentlichung des Bischöflichen Diözesanarchivs Aachen, 44), here 139-154.

[218] Reinhold, Korrespondenz 72 (Harreveld, 5. August 1878).

[219] Reinhold, Korrespondenz 78f. (Watersleyde, 19. April 1879).

Definitorium asked the General in July of 1873 to postpone the next Provincial Chapter for some time, due to the difficult circumstances of the *Kulturkampf*. Since 1870 a small group of Friars in the Province opposed the continuous change of leadership between Janknecht and Maasmann. Consequently, Janknecht cautiously chose to take no action in this affair himself. He left that to the Definitorium. This is how he tried to prevent accusations that he did not want to give up his office. The following year the Definitorium asked again for postponement. Transfers within the Province were not possible because of the laws of the *Kulturkampf*. Again, the initiative came officially from the Definitorium. In both cases the General approved the wishes of the Provincial leadership.[220] There are no sources indicating Janknecht's attitude towards this topic. It is likely that he tolerated the proposals. After all, he had to be willing to serve as Provincial. Furthermore, Janknecht probably had a great degree of influence on the Definitorium. Thus, it is unlikely that this body would have acted without the Provincial's consent. Janknecht's opinion was that continuity in Provincial leadership was beneficial in difficult times, as he indicated in a letter to the General Minister in December of 1875.[221]

In the summer of 1875 the Franciscans had to leave Prussia. Because of the difficult situation, Janknecht wrote to the General: "*The Chapter has to be postponed for a few weeks until the Friars have settled into the new houses in Holland and hopefully in Austria.*"[222] It was not before December 1875 that Janknecht asked the General for his instructions concerning the Provincial Chapter. He left no doubt that his time as Provincial would end with this Chapter.[223] However, Bernardino dal Vago did not support a Chapter at that time. Furthermore, he insisted that Janknecht should remain Provincial of Saxonia because there was nobody else who could lead the Province as effectively under these difficult circumstances. Janknecht answered

---

[220] Reinhold, Korrespondenz 50 (Remagen, 21. August 1874).

[221] „In der jüngsten Vergangenheit freilich, als die Aufhebung der Konvente bevorstand und das Unglück von allen Seiten auf die Provinz einbrach, wäre es Feigheit von mir gewesen, die Last einem anderen zu überlassen." Reinhold, Korrespondenz 59 (Harreveld, 28. December 1875).

[222] Reinhold, Korrespondenz 58 (Wien, 23. September 1875).

[223] Reinhold, Korrespondenz 58 (Harreveld, 11. Dezember 1875) and Reinhold, Korrespondenz 59 (Harreveld, 17. Dezember 1875)

the concerns from Rome in a detailed letter on December 28, 1875.[224] Janknecht did not want to give a false impression to his Friars. Therefore, he urged the General to tell the members of the Province that the decision about the Chapter and the Provincial had been made by the leadership of the Order. Besides that, he wanted to forestall his future critics—by attending to *"many unpleasant affairs such as the appointment of new Guardians. Since there are many fewer friaries than before, there will be fewer Guardians as well."*[225] It is not certain if Janknecht was really concerned about his reputation among the Friars or if he was exercising diplomatic skill. However, he calmed those Friars who preferred P. Vinzenz Halbfaß as Provincial and who had opposed Janknecht's and Maasmann's supremacy since 1870.[226]

On January 14, 1876, the Minister General appointed Janknecht by decree as Provincial for the next three years. The Definitorium was confirmed as well. Instead of Vinzenz Halbfaß, who lived in America, P. Severinus Orbach was appointed to the Definitorium as Janknecht had suggested before.[227] Janknecht promised *"to zealously lead the office entrusted to me and to take care of our mission during the next three years."*[228] The same year he traveled to America and stayed there for almost a year and a half. The trip must have been very strenuous for him. Upon his return to Holland, he wrote to the General that he had *"definitely decided to lay down my office. It is impossible for me to continue. I want to be liberated from the sorrows, difficulties and administrative duties."*[229] Janknecht was tired of office. The continuous burden of serving as Provincial had worn him down. It was not so much the amount of work, but much more the mental strain. During the past years he had had to make many difficult decisions. His decision to step down was finally decided in December 1877 by the repeated danger of being sued by the court. He held to his decisions even after the dangers no longer existed.[230]

---

[224] Reinhold, Korrespondenz 58-61 (Harreveld, 28. Dezember 1875).

[225] Reinhold, Korrespondenz 59 (Harreveld, 17. Dezember 1875).

[226] Reinhold, Korrespondenz 79 (Watersleyde, 19. April 1876).

[227] Reinhold, Korrespondenz 59-61 (Harreveld, 28. Dezember 1875), Fleckenstein, Franziskaner 41 and 330.

[228] Reinhold, Korrespondenz 61f. (Harreveld, 31. Januar 1876).

[229] Reinhold, Korrespondenz 69 (Cleveland, 22. Dezember 1877).

[230] Reinhold, Korrespondenz 69 (Cleveland, 22. Dezember 1877) and Reinhold, Korrespondenz 71 (Harreveld, 9. Mai 1878).

Furthermore, it seems that Janknecht was tortured by increasing doubts about himself. He apologized twice to the General for his *"failures, mistakes and imperfections during my term."*[231]

Following Janknecht's repeated pleas to be relieved of his office, the General Definitorium appointed new leadership for the Saxonian Province. In doing so, the General considered Janknecht's proposals, which were very important to him.[232] Janknecht proposed Maasmann for Provincial; accordingly, the General appointed him to this office on April 26, 1879. Ignatius Jeiler became Custos. Athanasius Kleinwächter, Georg Bartels, Ambrosius Dreimüller and Menander Gipperich were appointed as Definitors.[233] Janknecht was greatly relieved that he did not have to carry the burden of office anymore. *"I say many thanks to the Eternal Father for being released from the Provincial's office and that it has been put into such capable hands."*[234]

6. 1879-1888

The year 1879 marks a turning point in Janknecht's life. Since 1855 he had stood at the peak of the Province for 18 years. Moreover, he had been General Definitor for six years. Janknecht was sick of office and longed for some quiet years. The following chapter illuminates the mental consequences of the burdensome years.

6.1 *Praeses/Guardian in Harreveld and Remagen*

"I hope to be released from all offices. However, I was urged to lead this residence with 50 Friars."[235] Since many Friars had gone to America in the wake of the *Kulturkampf*, the Province in the Dutch exile was poorly staffed. Consequently, it could not spare an organizational talent such as Janknecht. He had spent the first years of the exile in Harreveld and liked the place. Thus, he was destined to become

---

[231] Reinhold, Korrespondenz 70 (Harreveld, 5. April 1878); and Reinhold, Korrespondenz 58 (Harreveld, 11. December 1875).

[232] Reinhold, Korrespondenz 79 (Watersleyde, 19. April 1879).

[233] Reinhold, Korrespondenz 70-80.

[234] Reinhold, Korrespondenz 80 (Harreveld, 9. Juli 1879).

[235] Reinhold, Korrespondenz 80 (Harreveld, 9. Juli 1879). Janknecht was unanimously elected as Guardian of Harreveld at the Provincial Chapter in Püth on May 15, 1879. Compare: ASFP Werl, Acta capitularia 1843-1888, 428, 435.

Guardian of the friary. Furthermore, he had always been very interested in new recruits. He had collected valuable experience as professor and as Master of Novices. Consequently, he was also appointed Professor of Humanistic Studies. He served in both offices until he left Harreveld in 1887.[236]

The first investment in Harreveld had taken place on November 29, 1875. After new candidates had enrolled in the novitiate in the spring of 1876, Harreveld became the new novitiate of the Saxonian Province in March 1876. These candidates had previously been students at the Seraphic College of the Province in Silesia. The foundation of this college had been initiated by Janknecht in 1870 on Mount St. Annaberg. The college was intended to recruit new members to the Order. It accepted only students who seriously wanted to enter the Order. Since it charged only an annual nutrition fee, even poor families could afford to provide their sons the higher education necessary for priesthood.[237] After the expulsion from Silesia, the College was at first relocated in Watersleyde. However, the residence there was dissolved in 1882, so that Janknecht relocated it in Harreveld after extensive construction was completed. He became Director of the College.[238] The house had space for approximately 50 students, who studied at the Grammar school for four years. This was a prerequisite to being enrolled in the Novitiate. With the College, Harreveld had gained an important position within the Province. This is the reason why the Friary was not closed after the Order returned to its Prussian friaries at the end of the 1880s. Instead, it was even expanded. In 1890 it received an additional wing so that 150 students could live there.[239] Since the students lived in a boarding-school, they gained an equivalent education and experienced Franciscan community life at the same time. Under

---

[236] Peters, *Totenbuch* II, 297. Janknecht was unanimously reelected at the Midterm-Chapters in Moresnet in 1880 and 1884 as well as at the Chapters in Moresnet in 1882 and in Kerkrade in 1885. ASFP Werl, Acta capitularia 1843-1888, 443, 445, 464, 489, 531.

[237] The Seraphic College later was a model for other German and European Provinces. Schlager, Patricius: Geschichte des Klosters Harreveld. In: *Festschrift zur Eröffnung des Kollegs der PP. Franziskaner St. Ludwig bei Dalheim (Rheinland) am 4. Oktober 1909.* (Münster, 1909), 16-38, here 35.

[238] ASFP Werl, Acta capitularia 1843-1888, 457, 471, 489.

[239] Fleckenstein, Franziskaner 62.

Janknecht's leadership the Novitiate developed as a model institution and the "Spirit of Harreveld" became proverbial.[240]

One of Janknecht's main duties was to choose new students for the College and to supervise the classes. Besides that he probably often had to make decisions which were not supposed to be his responsibility. One case is documented in Janknecht's letters. In this case the Provincial Maasmann left it to Janknecht to decide if the candidate Haselhoff should be permitted into the Novitiate.[241]

At the end of the 1870s the Prussian *Kulturkampf* started to lose its intensity. Bismarck realized that he could not achieve his goal. Furthermore, Socialism seemed an even greater threat to the Chancellor than the Catholic Church. This détente was encouraged by the new Pope Leo XIII, who had signaled his willingness to negotiate with Bismarck after his election in February 1878. Because of these circumstances, the Saxonian Franciscans were finally allowed to return to their friaries in Prussia in 1887.[242]

At the Provincial Chapter in Kerkrade in June 1887, Janknecht was recalled from Harreveld and appointed as Guardian of the Friary on Mount Apollinarisberg close to Remagen.[243] At first Janknecht was unsure about this step. In a letter to Döbbing he later wrote: "*As far as I am concerned, I am doing much better than I had thought and feared. We have love and peace, enough work, my relationship with P. Thomas [Klarholz] is relatively good and my health as well; I can do everything without effort. I pray and read at table. Praise to the Sacred Heart of Jesus and to the Most Blessed Virgin!*"[244] Probably, Janknecht's reluctance to move to Remagen had different roots. After a while in Prussia, he convinced himself that the repressions against the Catholic Church and especially against the Orders were really over.

[240] Fleckenstein, Franziskaner 321.

[241] ASFP Werl, Personalakte P. Gregor Janknecht (Harreveld, 9. Februar 1882). Generally, the Provincial had to decide about the permission of new candidates, compare: Fleckenstein, Franziskaner 88.

[242] Morsey, Kulturkampf 174-180. For the return of the Franciscans to Westfalia see: Häger, Peter: *Klöster nach dem Kulturkampf. Zur preußischen Genehmigungspolitik gegenüber den katholischen Männerorden in der Provinz Westfalen zwischen 1887 und 1919.* (Paderborn, 1997), especially 87-104.

[243] ASFP Werl, Acta capitularia 1843-1888, 559.

[244] ASFP Werl, Nachlaß Bernhard Döbbing, Janknecht an Döbbing (St. Apollinaris-berg, 12. November 1887).

A normal life was possible again. Furthermore, the *Kulturkampf* had not had decreased the need for pastoral work by the Franciscans. His difficulties with P. Thomas Klarholz were also quickly shattered.[245] The main reason for his reservations however was his health. In 1881 Janknecht had been diagnosed with a mental condition and was sent to a health resort in Kissingen. He was no longer capable of speaking or acting in public without experiencing panic attacks. This became so bad that the Provincial temporarily had to exclude him from prayer at table. Janknecht also had to cancel a visitation of the Belgian Province. Provincial Maasmann supported him in that decision since he feared that Janknecht might otherwise become unfit for any other office in the future.[246]

Three years later Janknecht again had to reject a visitation of the Belgian Province because of health reasons.[247] There is very little information about Janknecht's disease. Only a few hints in his personal letters allow the conclusion that his recovery progressed very slowly. He was able to fulfill his daily duties as Guardian of Harreveld after the first phase of the disease had run its course. Public appearances however were still difficult for him. For this time period, there are no significant actions of Janknecht recorded. In a letter from November 12, 1887, he notes that he had prayed at table again. This indicates that he had not been able to do so during the last few years or since the outbreak of his disease in 1881. By 1888 the disease seemed to be under control, so Janknecht was able to go on two trips. From May until July he stayed in Rome and supported Döbbing at St. Isidore. From August until September he visited the Irish Province as General Visitator.[248]

6.2 *Reformer of the Irish Province*

Soon after Janknecht had laid down the office of Provincial Minister, he was asked by the General to visit the Irish Province.

---

[245] Peters, *Totenbuch* II, 103.

[246] Reinhold, Korrespondenz 80f.

[247] Enneking, Pater Aloys Lauer *NF* 36 (1981) 251.

[248] Janknecht mentions the trips in a letter to his sister Hermine (Elisabeth) Janknecht dated December 10, 1888: Ich habe diesen Sommer und Herbst zwei ordentliche Reisen machen müssen (nach Rom von Mai bis Juli und Irland August u. September), die mir gut bekommen sind." ASFP Werl, Personalakte P. Gregor Janknecht (Warendorf, 10. Dezember 1888).

Thus, Janknecht and P. Irenaeus Bierbaum traveled to Ireland in September 1879. Janknecht had requested Bierbaum since he had lived in America for several years and spoke English fluently. Consequently, he could visit the Lay Brothers. Janknecht considered his own English too poor for this occasion.[249] The visitation of the Irish friaries revealed a devastating situation. The Saxonian Province was asked to support and advance the reform of the Irish Province, especially concerning the studies and discipline within the Order. Over the course of the next 15 years, Janknecht gave many suggestions for the reform of the Irish Province and also for the Irish College St. Isidore in Rome.[250]

The first important step towards the reform was P. Bernhard Döbbing's appointment as Professor of Theology at St. Isidore. He took up the position on November 3, 1883, being only 28 years old.[251] From then on Döbbing and Janknecht stayed in close correspondence until Janknecht's death.[252] Reinhold described their relationship as that of a "father and a son."[253] From September 1891 until fall of 1892 Janknecht was Commissioner of the Saxonian Province for the College of St. Isidore.[254] In this position he gave Döbbing much advice and promoted the reform of the Irish Province in the Definitorium. The German Province did not always unconditionally stand behind the reform of the Irish Province. Janknecht often acted behind or even against Provincial Bierbaum's authority.[255] Besides hints and advice for Döbbing, Janknecht's letters also contained direct rebukes. In a letter from Dublin, Janknecht wrote

---

[249] Reinhold, Korrespondenz 81.

[250] Conlan, *St. Isidore* 182.

[251] Conlan, *St. Isidore* 187. Concerning P. Bernhard Döbbing: see Kopp, Matthias: "Döbbing, Bernhard." In: *Lexikon für Theologie und Kirche. Bd. 3.* (Freiburg et al., 1995), Column 278 as well as Hardick, Lothar: Bischof Bernhard Döbbing (1855-1916). Ein deutscher Bischof in Italien. Seiner innerkirchlichen Reformtätigkeit und seine Intervention zu Gunsten der Christlichen Gewerkschaften. In: *Westfälische Zeitschrift 109* (1959) 144-195.

[252] Compare: ASFP Werl, Nachlaß Bernhard Döbbing, Janknecht an Döbbing 1883-1996. The first letter is dated from November 20, 1883.

[253] Reinhold, Übersicht 238.

[254] Reinhold, Übersicht 294 and ASFP Werl, Nachlaß Bernhard Döbbing, Janknecht an Döbbing (Paderborn, 22. November 1892).

[255] ASFP Werl, Nachlaß Bernhard Döbbing, Janknecht an Döbbing (St. Apollinarisberg 22. März 1888).

during his visitation: "*by the way, be careful with what you say or write to the Provincial. You know what I mean. Do not be mad at me when I remind you, that you have repeatedly lacked the necessary discretion in the past.*"[256] Besides that, Janknecht tried to calm Döbbing whenever possible: "*Most of all: Keep cool!*"[257] "*Remain quiet!*"[258]

Since Döbbing and his reforms were opposed by several members of the clergy, he wished to have some Friars from the Saxonian Province at the College of St. Isidore. They were supposed to serve as good examples to the Irish Friars. Consequently, Saxonia sent ten Clerics and Lay Brothers to St. Isidore. They arrived in December 1883 and the following summer were all chosen by Janknecht.[259] Two years later the Irish Novitiate temporarily moved from Ennis to Harreveld. The reform of the Province would be achieved by new recruits trained in the strict observance.[260]

The year of 1888 was a turning point in the reform of the Irish Province. Guardian Luke Carey stepped down from his office so that a successor had to be found. For this purpose, Janknecht traveled to St. Isidore to find out what the situation was.[261] In August he set off for his official Visitation of the Irish Province.[262] Janknecht had been appointed as General Visitator of the Irish Province despite its problems with the Saxonian Province during the past years.[263] The

[256] ASFP Werl, Nachlaß Bernhard Döbbing, Janknecht an Döbbing (Dublin, 25. August 1888).

[257] ASFP Werl, Nachlaß Bernhard Döbbing, Janknecht an Döbbing (St. Apollinarisberg, 24. April 1888).

[258] ASFP Werl, Nachlaß Bernhard Döbbing, Janknecht an Döbbing (St. Apollinarisberg, 15. Oktober 1888).

[259] Conlan, *St. Isidore* 188; Enneking, Pater Aloys Lauer *NF 36* (1981) 264.

[260] Enneking, Pater Aloys Lauer *NF 36* (1981) 264.

[261] ASFP Werl, Personalakte P. Gregor Janknecht (Warendorf, 10. Dezember 1888); also ASFP Werl, Nachlaß Bernhard Döbbing, Janknecht an Döbbing (St. Apollinarisberg, 10. August 1888).

[262] *Acta Ordinis Minorum* 7 (1888) 165.

[263] In March 1888 Janknecht remarked towards Döbbing: „Wenn ich den Auftrag des P. Rmus zur Visitation der irländ. Provinz bekomme, will ich im Vertrauen auf Gott ihn annehmen. Mehr kann ich nicht sagen. Die Sache sieht sich sehr trübe an. Und ob P. Rmus mit Rücksicht auf die jetzigen Spannung nicht doch einen anderen Visitator nimmt, ist auch noch eine Frage." ASFP Werl, Nachlaß Bernhard Döbbing, Janknecht an Döbbing (St. Apollinarisberg, 22. März 1888). Obviously, the General ordered Janknecht to go to Ireland only shortly before the Visitation. On August 10 he wrote to Döbbing: "P. Rmus schrieb mir von Parma aus, er wünsche trotzdem, daß

Visitation went well in Janknecht's opinion.[264] However, he was a bit insecure because the General did not answer his report for a long time.[265] His fears were groundless. Soon afterwards, the Minister General made several decisions concerning the Irish Province as a result of Janknecht's Visitation: The Novitiate was permanently moved to the Saxonian Province, which also received the authority over the two Irish friaries in Italy: Capranica and St. Isidore. Döbbing was appointed President of the College.[266] While the Irish still opposed the foundation of a Seraphic College during the Visitation of 1885,[267] it could now be established in Capranica near Rome. It was headed by Professors from the Saxonian Province.[268] Thus, the reform progressed under Döbbing's leadership, while Janknecht advised him. Finally, the first new Irish Friary was founded in Multyfarnham with Friars from the Italian Friaries in 1896. When Döbbing stepped down from his office as Guardian of St. Isidore, the reform of the Irish Province was finally completed.[269]

7. Provincial Minister 1888-1891

The Provincial Chapter of 1888 took place in Paderborn. It was headed by Aloysius Lauer, who had also visited the Province in advance. He had especially praised the College and the Novitiate as exemplary.[270] The Chapter elected Gregory Janknecht as Provincial on September 27. It was Janknecht's fifth term. The election was unambiguous. Janknecht received 14 votes, while the other candidates P.Basilius Pfannenschmid, P. Othmar Maasmann and P. Irenaeus Bierbaum received only one vote each.[271] The Provincial office was in

---

ich in Irland Visitation und Capitel halte." ASFP Werl, Nachlaß Bernhard Döbbing, Janknecht an Döbbing (St. Apollinarisberg, 10. August 1888).

[264] ASFP Werl, Nachlaß Bernhard Döbbing, Janknecht an Döbbing (St. Apollinarisberg, 23. September 1888).

[265] ASFP Werl, Nachlaß Bernhard Döbbing, Janknecht an Döbbing (St. Apollinarisberg, 15. Oktober 1888).

[266] Conlan, *St. Isidore* 194f.

[267] Enneking, Pater Aloys Lauer *NF 36* (1981) 263.

[268] Kordwittenborg, *Franziskanerprovinz* 40.

[269] Conlan, *St. Isidore* 206.

[270] Enneking, Pater Aloys Lauer *NF 36* (1981) 256-259.

[271] ASFP Werl, Acta capitularia 1843-1888, 595. See also: Acta Ordinis Minorum 7 (1888) 166.

Warendorf, where Janknecht lived for the following three years.[272] Janknecht obviously no longer feared the responsibility of the office. There is no word of it in his letters anymore.

The Chapter decided to staff the residences in Bonn and Monchengladbach as soon as possible. From October 4 all Friars would wear their habit again and observe the Rule in the friaries. Furthermore, the Provincial Statutes and the Ceremonies were supposed to be revised until the next Midterm Chapter. All these measures are attempts of the Provincial leadership to reestablish the Order after the return from the exile.[273] The residences were staffed the next year as planned. The construction of a new friary in Monchengladbach was started in 1890. Finally, the State gave permission for a new friary in Cologne which was officially opened on October 15, 1890.[274] Besides these new foundations there were various offers for the Franciscans to establish new friaries in new cities. None of these was initiated by the Province. The members of the Chapter however did not want to act rashly and therefore postponed their decisions until the next Chapter. Since it was not certain that there would be enough Priests to staff these residences, the Province preferred to wait.[275]

The main focus of his term however was on the General Chapter in which Janknecht participated as Provincial Minister.[276] For the first time, the Chapter took place in the new St. Anthony College in Rome. The Chapter especially emphasized the revision of the General Statutes. The General aimed at the adoption of new Statutes which would be obligatory for all reform groups. He established a special commission for this goal. The commission consisted of nine Patres under the leadership of Aloys Lauer, Janknecht being one of them.[277]

Consequently, Janknecht was especially in demand during the Chapter. The discussions about this topic lasted from September 24

---

[272] ASFP Werl, Acta capitularia 1843-1888, 606 as well as ASFP Werl, Acta capitularia 1890-1921, 7.

[273] Enneking, Pater Aloys Lauer NF 36 (1981) 257; Fleckenstein, Franziskaner 67.

[274] Schmies / Rakemann, *Spuren* 509, 511.

[275] Fleckenstein, Franziskaner 69, 82f.

[276] *Capitulum Generale totius Ordinis Fratrum Minorum S.P.N. Francisci Romae in ven. Collegio S. Antonimi Patavini die 3 octobris 1889 celebratum.* Quaracchi 1890, here 27. See also: *Acta Ordinis Minorum* 8 (1889) 176.

[277] *Capitulum Generale 1889,* 16f.; *Acta Ordinis Minorum* 8 (1889) 173f.; Enneking, Pater Aloys Lauer NF 36 (1981) 248f.

until October 10 before they were concluded successfully. The new General Statutes were proclaimed in April 1890 and printed the same year.[278] These were the first Statutes since 1517 which were obligatory for the whole Order. This was also an important step towards the unification of the different reform families and it was continued at the next General Chapter in Assisi in 1895. Besides the joint legislation, the leadership under the General and one Procurator over the whole Order would be guaranteed. These foundations of the Union were accepted by a large majority of the General Definitorium in Assisi. In a secret ballot, 77 participants of the Chapter voted for it, with only 31 against. Consequently, Pope Leo XIII endorsed the unification of the different families on October 4, 1897 through the constitution *Felicitate quadam*. The Conventuals and the Capuchins were not involved in this decision. From then on, the observant families all carried the title Ordo Fratrum Minorum and were subordinate to the same legislation and leadership of the Order. The uniform brown habit was compulsory for all Friars. Aloys Lauer was appointed as first Minister General of the Union.[279] Initially, Janknecht had also been considered for this office. However, he died in 1896. Loddenkötter correctly assumes that the Saxonian Provincial Minister had been in favor of the new General Statutes since he had worked in their commission.[280] This attitude also becomes clear in one of his letters from the year 1893. However he also expresses doubts about the lasting success of this enterprise: "*I regard it as very likely that the familiae will no longer exist in the Order and that the fusio will become reality. The Cardinal said that outside Italy there is support or at least no opposition. I only know of 3-4 opponents in our own Province and I do not consider them very strong. I think the same is true for the other Provinces that I know. However, there may be different views whether the fusio will last permanently and unite the whole Order.*"[281]

---

[278] *Constitutiones Generales Ordinis Minorum a Capitulo Generali Romae in Collegio Sancti Antonii Patavini anno 1889 celebrato revisae et approbatae iussus et auctoritate Rmi P. Alysii a Parma Ministri Generalis totius Ordinis Minorum publicatae.* (Quaracchi, 1890).

[279] Holzapfel, *Handbuch* 374-379; Schmies / Rakemann, *Spuren* 515, 517, 519.

[280] Loddenkötter, *P. Gregor* 219.

[281] ASFP Werl, Nachlaß Bernhard Döbbing, Janknecht an Döbbing (Paderborn, 19. April 1893).

Shortly after the General Chapter, the General Definitorium appointed Janknecht on November 28, 1889 as Commissioner of the Holy Land for all of Germany except Bavaria.[282] The Commissioner's main task was to collect money for the schools and missions in the Holy Land.[283] This office was initiated by the Minister General dal Vago at the Provincial Chapter in 1888 at the request of Saxonia. At this time, it was rejected, since the Provincial was supposed to fulfill this task within his duties.[284] Since Janknecht was also Provincial when he was appointed Commissioner, the Province finally received its favorite constellation. After the new General Constitution of 1890 it was no longer allowed to unite the office of the Provincial Minister and the General Commissioner in one person. Still, Janknecht received a telegraphic dispensation from Rome,[285] perhaps because he had been appointed as General Commissioner only a few months before. After the end of his Provincial term in September 1891, he remained General Commissioner for the Holy Land until his death in 1896.[286]

8. Guardian in Harreveld and Paderborn 1891-1896

Janknecht's last term as Provincial ended at the Provincial Chapter on September 24, 1891. He and Maasmann were the only candidates at the election. While Janknecht received only five votes, Maasmann was elected by twelve votes on the first ballot. Even in the election for the Custos, Janknecht was not able to assert himself against P. Benedictus Bechte. However, he was elected Guardian of Paderborn,[287] which he only held until the next Midterm Chapter in 1893. There he became Guardian of the Friary in Harreveld, which

---

[282] *Acta Ordinis Minorum* 8 (1889) 190.

[283] Holzapfel, *Handbuch* 552.

[284] Enneking, P. Aloys Lauer 257f.

[285] Fleckenstein, Franziskaner 332.

[286] *Acta Ordinis Minorum* 15 (1896) 60. Peters, *Totenbuch* II, 239 only mentions the years 1891 until 1896. This is wrong. ASFP Werl, Acta capitularia 1890-1921, 70 and 89.

[287] ". . . of course unanimously. . ." as he writes to Döbbing; ASFP Werl, Nachlaß Bernhard Döbbing, Janknecht an Döbbing (Warendorf, 2. Oktober 1891).

[288] ASFP Werl, Acta capitularia 1890-1921, 35, 47, 49 and 70. See also Schmies / Rakemann, *Spuren* 511 and 513.

had been elevated to a convent in 1891.[288] Janknecht served there until March 1896. Shortly before his death, he was elected as Guardian of Remagen again.[289]

Even though Janknecht's term as Provincial had officially ended in 1891, he served as a deputy for Maasmann several times during the following years because he was often sick.[290] Moreover, Maasmann appointed him as his Commissioner for St. Isidore and the mission in Brazil,[291] so that Janknecht was still very busy. Probably, Janknecht preferred to return to Harreveld in 1891. The friary and especially the College meant so much to him. In the resume of his last term, he writes: *"The goal at my election was to build up and secure Harreveld. At the end of the three years, the number of students has doubled and every-thing is paid—no debts. Soli Deo gratia!"*[292] Consequently, he was ini-tially reluctant to move to Paderborn. His concerns however were without reason. In March of 1892 he wrote: *"As far as I am concerned, it was not easy for me to accept the Guardianship of Paderborn. However, I feel at home by now and my health is doing fine."*[293]

In 1892 the preparations for the foundation of the Friary S. Elia, located 40 kilometers north of Rome, were finished. Bishop Constantini, who was responsible for the building, had been looking in vain for a religious community to maintain the local picture of Mary and the place of pilgrimage. In April 1891 he accidentally met Janknecht, who was on a pilgrimage to the grotto of S. Elia during his stay in Capranica.[294] After that, Janknecht and Döbbing decided to establish a friary, which could serve as a summer residence for the Irish Friars in Italy. Since the Seraphic College had been opened in

---

[289] ASFP Werl, Acta capitularia 1890-1921, 102, 108.

[290] Loddenkötter, P. Gregor 222. There are several hints in his letters to Döbbing for Janknecht deputizing Maasmann. The first time was already three weeks after Maasmann's election. ASFP Werl, Nachlaß Bernhard Döbbing, Janknecht an Döbbing (Warendorf, 2. Oktober 1891).

[291] ASFP Werl, Nachlaß Bernhard Döbbing, Janknecht an Döbbing (Warendorf, 2. Oktober 1891).

[292] Werl, Nachlaß Bernhard Döbbing, Janknecht an Döbbing (Paderborn, 3. Mai 1892).

[293] Werl, Nachlaß Bernhard Döbbing, Janknecht an Döbbing (Paderborn, 8. März 1892).

[294] Probably, this trip was connected with the opening of the Seraphic College in Capranica.

Capranica, there was not enough space anymore for this purpose. In January of 1892, Döbbing asked the General for permission to establish the new residence and it was granted a few months later. In July 1892, the first Franciscans went to S. Elia. The place of pilgrimage experienced a massive uplift under Döbbing's leadership.[295] The path to the successful establishment of the friary however was not easy.[296] Finally, Janknecht managed to convince the Provincial leadership of the Saxonia to support Döbbing's project.

After S. Elia had been successfully founded, another shrine in Italy was entrusted to the Saxonian Franciscans. Janknecht and Döbbing were received by Pope Leo XIII on Ash Wednesday 1894. The Pope had already asked Döbbing in 1893 and now renewed his plea that they take on the Church of Mary in Amaseno, close to Naples. The Church had fallen into disrepair and the Franciscans were supposed to restore the place of pilgrimage. At first there was opposition from the Saxonian Province, but later it dissipated. The Friary was founded by Saxonian Franciscans in 1896. In 1907 however, it was given up.[297]

In March 1895 Janknecht's longtime companion, Othmar Maasmann, died. They had worked closely together since their days in the Novitiate. From 1855 until 1894 they had led the Province together with only a short interruption from 1885 until 1888. They came from the same generation of Franciscans and pursued similar goals during their Provincial terms. This was an important reason for Saxonia's enormous growth in the second half of the 19th century. Consequently, it is no wonder that Maasmann's death deeply affected

[295] Conlan, *St. Isidore* 201-203; Scheiwe, Friedhelm: 80 Jahre Franziskaner in Castel S. Elia. In: *Vita Seraphica* 53 (1972) 180-190; Lemmens, Leonhard: Das Franziskanerkloster zu Castel St. Elia. In: *Franziskanische Studien* 7 (1920) 241-247; especially 244f.; Kirsch, J.P.: „Castel Sant'Elia." In: *Lexikon für Theologie und Kirche.* (Freiburg/Br., 1931), Column 788.

[296] Werl, *Nachlaß Bernhard Döbbing*, Janknecht an Döbbing (Warendorf, 2. Oktober 1891 / Paderborn, 8. März 1892, Paderborn, 10. März 1892 / Paderborn, 28. März 1892 / Paderborn, 18. Juni 1892).

[297] Kullmann, P. Gregor 57f.; Loddenkötter, P. Gregor 222; Schmies / Rakemann, Spuren 517. Janknecht's letters to Döbbing describe the development of the Friary in Amaseno. ASFP Werl, Nachlaß Bernhard Döbbing, Janknecht an Döbbing (between Harreveld, 3. November 1893 and Harreveld, 26. Dezember 1894). Also Reinhold, Übersicht 238.

Janknecht. He not only told Döbbing about his feelings[298] but mentioned it even to his benefactors: "*At the same time a terrible suffering occurred to me through the death of P. Othmarus, who had been a dear Confrater and close friend for 46 years.*"[299]

8.1 *The Mission in Brazil*[300]

There had been two Franciscan Provinces in Brazil since the 17th century, one in the North and one in the South of the country. At the end of the 19th century, both Provinces stood at the verge of extinction because of the difficult political situation. To prevent this, the Provincial of the Northern St. Anthony Province, Antonio de S. Camillo de Lelles le Carvalho, asked the leadership of the Order for help. When the General Chapter discussed this topic in Assisi in 1889, it was Janknecht who offered to take over the Mission in Brazil. Consequently, Minister General Aloysius Canali de Parma transferred the mission territory to the Saxonian Province on December 18, 1889. In order to recruit the new Friars necessary for the mission, Janknecht turned the College in Harreveld into a Mission College.[301] However, due to the insecure political conditions in Brazil, the first Missionaries could not be sent there before May 1891. Janknecht, whom the Provincial had appointed as Commissioner for Brazil,[302] at first intended to accompany those first Friars on their journey to South America. Later, he changed his mind. P. Amandus Bahlmann led the group instead. Nevertheless, Janknecht wrote a long letter in June of 1892 to encourage the Friars.[303]

In 1893 the Definitorium asked Janknecht to travel to Brazil. However, the trip was postponed again and again. Finally, a few

---

[298] "*Sie können sich denken, wie mich der Tod des unvergeßlichen P. Othmarus angegriffen*"; Reinhold, Aus Briefen 298.

[299] ASFP Werl, Personalakte P. Gregor Janknecht (Paderborn, 14. April 1895).

[300] The chapters about the missions in North America and Brazil can only be given a short overview in this essay. There will be a more detailed study about these topics in the volume about the missions in the History of the Province which will be edited by Dieter Berg.

[301] Loddenkötter, P. Gregor 226, note 74.

[302] Reinhold, Aus Briefen 294.

[303] Janknecht, Gregor: Ermutigung in den Schwierigkeiten des Anfangs. Brief an die Brüder in der Brasilien Mission vom 6. Juni 1892. In: *Vita Seraphica* 75 (1994) 189-192.

weeks before his departure, Provincial Maasmann decided that instead of Janknecht, P. Irenaeus Bierbaum should go to Brazil for two years as Commissioner. Janknecht, who had previously voiced his concerns about such a long and difficult trip because of his age, accepted this change: "*With regard to my age and constitution, that would not be possible for me.*"[304] Nevertheless, more and more problems arose in the mission so that Janknecht was appointed as General Visitator of the Brazilian mission in 1895 at the age of 66. In April of 1895 he wrote to Döbbing: "*It seems to me that I am facing an almost certain death.*"[305] On June 6, 1895, Janknecht departed for Brazil together with P. Serapion Märzheuser. After his arrival in Bahia on June 25, he started the Visitation of the friaries in the North and then in the South. When he was finished, he wrote an extensive report for the Provincial Minister P. Basilius Pfannenschmid. This report gives a clear impression of the internal and external condition of the Brazilian mission.[306] Janknecht stayed longer in Brazil than planned: "*I have decided to stay here for an indefinite time, in order to calm and stabilize the condition here.*"[307] He stayed until February 1896 before he went back to Germany. The day of his departure, he signed a circular letter to the Friars in the Brazilian Mission, which remained current for many years since it contained fundamental orders for life in the mission.[308] Janknecht left the mission in a secure condition so that the two Brazilian Provinces—the Province of Immaculate Conception in the South and the St. Anthony Province in the North—could be officially reestablished in September 1901.[309]

During the return voyage in February 1896, Janknecht became seriously ill. He hardly reached Paderborn on February 27, where the Provincial Chapter was in session. He was so sick that he could not tell about his Visitation. He died on March 1—perhaps of the Yellow Fever he had caught in Brazil. The requiem mass was cele-

---

[304] Reinhold, Aus Briefen 296. Also Reinhold, Aus Briefen 295.

[305] Reinhold, Aus Briefen 298.

[306] Under the title: „Gegenwärtiger äußerer Befund und innerer Zustand der Franziskaner-Mission in Brasilien," Translation in Griesenbrock, P. Gregor 13-16.

[307] Reinhold, Aus Briefen 300.

[308] The circular letter from February 5, 1896 is printed in several sources. The last translation in Griesenbrock, P. Gregor 17-20.

[309] Schmies / Rakemann, *Spuren* 525.

brated by the Bishop of Paderborn, Dr. Hubert Simar. Janknecht was buried at the Eastern Cemetery in Paderborn.[310] When he died, the Saxonian Province of the Holy Cross consisted of 28 Friaries and more than 700 Friars. Thus, it had grown from its simple beginnings after Secularization to one of the largest Provinces of the Order, largely due to Janknecht's efforts.

9. Conclusion

Looking at Gregory Janknecht's life is like looking at the History of the Saxonian Province in the second half of the 19th century. The person Janknecht and the development of the Province are so closely connected. 21 years as Provincial Minister and almost 40 years as a member of the Definitorium left behind clear traces and show Janknecht's influence on the Province. It was due mainly to his organizational talents that the Province was strengthened after Secularization and revived the strict Observance. He particularly promoted new recruits in the Seraphic Colleges—especially in Harreveld—so that the Province also grew in personnel. His thoughtful actions during the *Kulturkampf* strengthened the Saxonian Province even during that difficult period. Finally, his love for the mission enabled the establishment and revival of several Provinces in North America and Brazil.

While still in his early thirties, he had already been involved in the leadership of the Order as General Definitor. Later, he contributed to the unification of the different reform families in the Order. Furthermore, he was appointed as General Visitator to various Provinces ten times. He successfully conducted eight of these Visitations to the Saxonian Province, North America, Brazil and the Irish Province. The Irish Province experienced an extensive reform because of his Visitation.

This list gives a hint of the physical and psychological pressures Janknecht was subjected to during his life. Consequently, it is no wonder that he became seriously ill after the end of the *Kulturkampf* and needed several years to recover. But it also shows that

---

[310] Loddenkötter, P. Gregor 227, note 79; *Festschrift zum 300jährigen Bestehen des Franziskanerklosters* Paderborn, 329.

Janknecht's life had almost entirely been a "success story." He knew how to pursue and to achieve his goals. He was strong willed, which some Friars took exception to. He also used his good standing with the leadership of the Order to achieve his goals. Janknecht's comprehensive correspondence, which contains many personal letters, reveal the motivations behind his actions. At the same time, they also give an impression of the person of Gregory Janknecht—belying Kullmann's opinion, that "*it is impossible to give an adequate picture of the personality of Pater Gregory with all its bright and dark sides.*"[311] In the end, Janknecht was a child of his age, shaped by the piety and attitudes of the Catholic Church in the 19th century, but also helping to shape and define his age.

---

[311] ASFP Werl, Personal File of P. Gregory Janknecht; letter from P. Willibald Kullmann to P. Manfred Loddenkötter, Düsseldorf March 10, 1930.

The Exile of the Saxonian Franciscans in the United States During the Prussian *Kulturkampf*

By Stephan Scherfenberg

On June 3, 1875, the Provincial of the Saxonian Province of the Holy Cross, Gregory Janknecht (O.S.F.), wrote hopefully to his confreres: "*We are confident that this persecution will not lead to the expected decline of our Province, but rather to the promotion and spread of the Kingdom of God.*"[1] Only three days before, the Prussian Parliament had passed the *Klostergesetz*. This law forbade the Franciscans and other Catholic Orders to work or to stay in Prussia. It was followed by the exodus of thousands of clergymen and seminarians, among them about 400 Franciscans from the Saxonian Province. One hundred twenty-six of these came to the US.

At this time, the Franciscans were not the only Germans emigrating to the United States. During the 1830s a steady stream of immigrants began arriving, reaching its climax in 1854, when 220,000 German immigrants arrived in US ports.[2] Another wave of immigrants began in 1880. A million and a half people left the German Empire during the decade 1880-1890—more than in any other decade before or after. Immigration slowed significantly after the turn of the century, when German industry gained enough strength to hire the many people who had lost their occupations in the chang-

---

[1] Janknecht to the Minister General, June 3, 1875 (Reinhold, Julius: Aus der römischen Korrespondenz des P. Gregor Janknecht über die Jahre 1871-1879. In: *Vita Seraphica* 29 [1948] 47-82, here 54).

[2] Wolfgang Helbich, *Alle Menschen sind dort gleich... Die deutsche Amerika-Auswanderung im 19. und 20. Jahrhundert* (Düsseldorf, 1988), 18f.

ing economy.[3] In sum, between 1820 and 1920 about 5.5 million Germans emigrated to the US.[4]

The reasons for this heavy migration are as different as the individuals involved, although the majority came for classic economic reasons—to live a better life. Most immigrants set off full of hope but then experienced a difficult Atlantic crossing, followed by years of privation and hard work. Germans had to establish themselves in a new land, settling in near primitive conditions. Many had to rely entirely on themselves. The rural community they had known in Europe, where everybody looked after everyone else, was difficult to reestablish in the United States. Here, immigrants found a different culture to which they could either adapt or try to remain distinct. Should they continue to speak German or abandon their native tongue and speak English? Some habits and traditions were abandoned, while others were preserved. Immigrants brought cherished ideals, values and specific social behaviors from their homeland and struggled to adapt or preserve them in this new environment.[5]

The Franciscans experienced the same difficulties other immigrants did. In addition, life in America also brought them into conflict with their Rule and the European leadership of the Order. How did the Friars cope with the challenges in their new homeland? Where did they adapt and where did they resist the pressures of acculturation? Did they behave differently than the other immigrants? Did their connection with the Order and the Rule help them to cope more easily with the challenges of the New World?

1. What Forced the Franciscans into Exile?

The primary reason for the Saxonian Franciscans' journey to America was the *Kulturkampf* (Culture War) in Prussia. In June 1872 the Jesuits were the first Catholic Order to be expelled from the German Empire. In May 1875 all other Orders were banished. The first paragraph of the *Klostergesetz* (Convent Law) says:

---

[3] Willi Adams, *Deutsche im Schmelztiegel der USA* (Berlin, 1994), 6.

[4] Helbich, *Menschen* 19.

[5] Johannes Paulmann, „Internationaler Vergleich und interkultureller Transfer. Zwei Forschungsansätze zur europäischen Geschichte des 18. bis 20. Jahrhunderts," in *Historische Zeitschrift*, Lothar Gall (Ed.), Vol. 267 (München, 1998), 673-680.

*"All Orders and similar congregations of the Catholic Church are expelled
from the territory of the Prussian Monarchy. They are no longer allowed to
maintain convents. Existing convents are not allowed to accept new members and have to be dissolved within six months after the proclamation of
the law."*[6]

With this law the legislation of the *Kulturkampf* reached its climax.
Consequently, by 1880, 1,770 Catholic priests and all but three
Bishops were either expelled from Prussia, imprisoned or had to
leave their Orders. Over 1,200 clergymen and 7,763 nuns were
driven out of their convents. 1,200 parishes with more than two million people were left without a spiritual shepherd.[7]

The Franciscans of the Holy Cross Province were equally affected
by these repressive measures and had to leave Prussia. Under the
leadership of Provincial Gregory Janknecht, the Province had just
begun to recover from the effects of the secularization which had
beset them since the beginning of the 19th century, when the repressive measures of the *Kulturkampf* began.[8] The correspondence
between Janknecht and the Minister General Bernardino dal Vago da
Portugruaro suggests that for a number of years, the Province recognized portents of the coming suppression. Janknecht describes the
individual laws, their consequences for the Province and explains his
preparations for the evacuation of the friaries.

The Province felt the first direct consequences of the new laws in
December 1872 when P. Basilius Pfannenschmid was forbidden to
inspect the local school in Hardenberg-Neviges. One month before,
Janknecht had already expressed his concerns in a letter to the
General.[9] *"We do not know what our fate will be. But in the meantime, I
have written to Rome and asked for papal dispensation that we may sell*

---

[6] Johannes B. Kissling: *Geschichte des Kulturkampfes im deutschen Reich* (Freiburg,
1911-1916), Vol. 3, 440.

[7] See: Marion A. Habig (O.F.M.), *Heralds of the King: Franciscan Province of the
Sacred Heart* (Chicago 1958), 104.

[8] Because of secularization the number of Friars had declined drastically. Moreover,
the separation of the Alcantarines at the middle of the century had cost additional manpower. Young priests especially had left the Province. Kirsten Rakemann: „Gregor
Janknecht. Fünfmaliger Provinzialminister zwischen 1855 und 1891," in *Management
und Minoritas. Lebensbilder Sächsischer Franziskanerprovinziale vom 13. bis 20.
Jahrhundert*, Saxonia Franciscana Beiheft, Dieter Berg (Hrsg.), (Kevelar, 2003), 215.

[9] Rakemann, Janknecht, 231f.

the convents and our property if necessary."[10] Soon afterwards the General Procurator confirmed the papal dispensation. On January 13, 1873, Janknecht reported to the General that he would make use of this faculty only in the most extreme emergency.[11] After the May Laws of 1873 he wrote to the General, that all bishops, priests and Friars were threatened by persecution.[12] Janknecht tried to draw as little government attention to his Province as possible,[13] but on September 12, 1874, he reported that P. Thomas Klarholz from Remagen was forbidden to perform any pastoral work. Consequently, Janknecht had to help out with the confessions there because there was such a large crowd and so few Friar-priests.[14] Soon afterwards the friaries in Hardenberg, Düsseldorf and Remagen were forbidden to collect alms. The friaries in Paderborn, Werl and Rietberg were likewise searched.[15] In the spring of 1875 several Friars of the Province were called before a court because of their pastoral work. Since their appearance at court would have meant an acceptance of the laws, the defendants did not show up. Two of the priests were sentenced in their absence to three days in prison.[16]

This development caused Janknecht to look for alternative houses for the Friars in case the Order was expelled from Prussia. At first he made efforts to establish three friaries in the Bohemian Province. In addition, he wanted to establish three or four houses in Holland right at the Prussian border. The younger Friars, and indeed everyone who was capable, he proposed to send to the United States to support the American mission.[17] The establishment of new houses and the Friars' travel to the United States promised enormous debt for the Province. Therefore, Janknecht asked the General for a dispensation from the Franciscan Rule to collect money.[18] Moreover, he asked permission

---

[10] Janknecht to General Nov. 11, 1872, Reinhold, Korrespondenz, 48.

[11] Janknecht to General Jan. 13, 1873, Reinhold, Korrespondenz, 48.

[12] Janknecht to General May 16, 1873, Reinhold, Korrespondenz, 49.

[13] Rakemann, Janknecht, 232.

[14] Janknecht to General Sept. 12, 1874, Reinhold, Korrespondenz, 50.

[15] Janknecht to General Nov. 14, 1874, Reinhold, Korrespondenz, 50f.

[16] Janknecht to General March 23, 1875, March 31, 1875 and April 4, 1875, Reinhold, Korrespondenz, 52. See also Rakemann, Janknecht, 232.

[17] Janknecht to General April 4, 1875, April 23, 1875 and May 6, 1875, Reinhold, Korrespondenz, 53.

[18] Janknecht to General May 6, 1875, Reinhold, Korrespondenz, 53.

to allow some Friars to wear secular clothes and to use money. These Friars were supposed to stay in the friaries and look after them since the government had forbidden the sale of friaries. Consequently, to circumvent this law, the Franciscans rented their friaries for 10 or 15 years to benefactors of the Order. The Minister General agreed to all of these requests.[19]

Immediately after the proclamation of the *Klostergesetz*, Janknecht begged the Austrian Emperor Franz Josef I for permission to relocate his Friars to the Bohemian Province. Janknecht described the situation in his Province to the monarch. Out of 400 Friars, about 100 could go to the US, and about 200 could be accommodated in Holland. However since Holland was only partly Catholic, there were insufficient ministerial possibilities for priests. Janknecht also travelled to Vienna and Prague to negotiate with the local Provincial there. In the end, his endeavours failed.[20] The Franciscan Order would not be unified until 1897, so various members of the Franciscan family often remained independent of one another. This independence was also evident in the different groups of Franciscans settling in North America.[21]

While Janknecht was still in Austria, the Saxonian Friars had already begun to leave their friaries. On September 23, 1875, Janknecht wrote to the General: *"The Prussian government acted more severely against us than against the Jesuits, for it had given them half a year to move out."*[22] Janknecht could not even return to Germany, but had to go directly into exile in Dutch Harreveld. He founded several several houses close to the border and determined that this is where the Friars should be located. The elderly and infirm Friars especially should move to the neighbouring countries. The Dorsten Friary moved to Beezel, Rietberg and Warendorf to Harreveld, Wieden-brück to Brunsum, Paderborn to Püth, Düsseldorf to Bleyerheide and Aachen to Moresnet.[23] In fact almost all Westphalian friaries were relocated into Dutch territory.

---

[19] Janknecht to General June 3, 1875, Reinhold, Korrespondenz, 54.

[20] Gisela Fleckenstein, *Die Franziskaner im Rheinland 1875-1918* (Werl, 1992), 56-57.

[21] Compare: Dominic V. Monti (O.F.M.), "Franciscan Friars," in *Encyclopedia of American Catholic History*, Michael Glazier / Thomas J. Shelly (eds), (Collegeville, 1997), 526.

[22] Janknecht to General Sept. 23, 1875, Reinhold, Korrespondenz, 58.

[23] Janknecht to General Sept. 23, 1875, Reinhold,Korrespondenz, 57.

For the most part these rented properties were either cottages, small castles, or farms fallen into disrepair; here the Franciscans could make their simple homes. Many Germans crossed the border and came to these new friaries to confess their sins. In addition, there were also German-speaking Catholic parishes in Holland, such as in Bleyerheide. Thus, the Franciscans helped out there with the pastoral work.[24] In November 1875 the new novitiate was established in Harreveld. This enabled the Order to accept and educate new members. Janknecht was intent on re-establishing the daily routine of the Order as soon as possible. Obedience to the Rule and Statutes was paramount. This is why he refused to allow the Friars from Düsseldorf to leave the Order and to continue their parish work as secular priests.[25] It was important to Janknecht that the Friars preserve the observance of the Rule that had existed in the Saxonian Province. He expected his confreres to live their lives in accordance to the Rule—even in exile.[26]

In 1858, long before the *Kulturkampf*, the Saxonian Province had founded a mission in North America. By the year 1875 this mission consisted of six friaries, a novitiate and study houses. During the *Kulturkampf* these houses offered both accommodation and ministry for numerous Saxonian Franciscans. Since there was a constant need for German speaking priests, novices and especially priests were sent to the New World. In the end, all Friars fit to travel, were sent to the US, because there was not enough room in the Dutch and Belgian friaries. The Friars were free to decide to stay in their homeland or to go to America. Most of them went to the United States.

Many Franciscans interpreted their exile from the perspective of the Franciscan missionary ideal. The voyage to the United States was not so much regarded as expulsion from their hostile homeland, but rather as the departure into a new missionary undertaking. In this sense, Provincial Janknecht wrote to the General in Rome:

> *"By Divine Providence we have had a Mission in North America already since 1858. There the harvest is rich and the workers are few. Consequently, there is nothing better than to send as many of our Friars to help there and not withdraw from the command of obedience."*[27]

---

[24] Fleckenstein, Franziskaner, 58-63.

[25] Janknecht to General Nov. 11, 1875, Reinhold, Korrespondenz, 58.

[26] Rakemann, Janknecht, 235.

[27] Janknecht to General June 6, 1875, Reinhold, Korrespondenz, 54.

2. The North American Mission in the 1850s

At the time of their expulsion from Prussia, there were already around 100 Saxonian Franciscans in the North American Mission. Their influence so far was rather limited, being restricted to small towns and settlements of German and Polish immigrants. In the 19th century, the stewardship of the North American Catholic Church was largely in the hands of Irish bishops.[28] These bishops may have possessed a passionate zeal, but their ears were only partly open to the needs and wishes of the German-speaking Catholics. In 1846, only two out of 25 American bishops were of German descent. King Ludwig I of Bavaria supported German Catholics in the US with his Ludwig Missions Foundation. In addition, he used his influence in Rome to promote the appointment of more German bishops for the United States. That is one reason why more and more American dioceses came to have German speaking bishops. Still there were not enough priests to meet the pastoral needs of the German Catholic community. Consequently, many bishops travelled to Germany to recruit German-speaking priests for work in their diocese.[29] When Bishop Damian Juncker from Alton, Illinois was on his way back from Rome, he travelled through the North German dioceses in March of 1858. There were about 55,000 German Catholics in his extensive diocese in the State of Illinois,[30] but only 28 priests.[31] Bishop Conrad Martin of Paderborn referred him to Janknecht, then Provincial of the Saxonian Holy Cross Province.

Even though his Province was still weak from the effects of Secularization, Janknecht immediately agreed to send friars to Illinois after he consulted the Definitorium. Janknecht was very keen

[28] Michael Hochgeschwender, *Wahrheit, Einheit, Ordnung. Der US-amerikanische Katholizismus und die Sklavenfrage 1835-1870* (Tübingen, 2003), 52f.

[29] Georg Timpe, *Katholisches Deutschtum in den Vereinigten Staaten von Amerika. Ein Querschnitt* (Freiburg, 1957), 34f.

[30] P. Bonaventura Hammer (O.S.F.), *Die katholische Kirche in den Vereinigten Staaten* (New York, 1897), 357.

[31] See Siehe: *Annals of the Franciscan Province of the Sacred Heart* (St. Louis, 1929), Band 1, S. 3. These recruitment trips to Europe were very common in 19th century. Also in: Kathleen Neils Conzen, "German Catholics in America," in: Michael Glazier, Thomas J. Shelly (Ed.): *Encyclopedia of American Catholic History* (Collegeville, 1997), 571-583, here 576.

on the mission throughout his entire life. Originally, he had planned to go to the Chinese mission after his ordination. However, the difficult personnel situation in the Saxonian Province foiled this plan.[32] After his consultation with the Definitorium and the Minister General in Rome, Janknecht placed three priests, four Brothers and two Tertiaries at the disposal of the mission. Thus, the following Friars started their trip to North America on August 24, 1858:

- P. Damian Hennewig, 50 years old, leader of the group, Guardian of the Friary in Paderborn and Vice Provincial.
- P. Johannes Capistran Zwinge, 35 years old, lived in the Friary in Annaberg for several years, he was shaped by the most radical Franciscan ideals and a dedicated missionary.
- P. Servatius Altmicks, 29 years old, he would become known for his numerous foundations of friaries and his work among the Indians.
- Br. Irenaeus Drewes, 36 years old, carpenter.
- Br. Paschalis Kutsche, 37 years old, tailor.
- Br. Marianus Beile, 32 years old, gardener.
- Br. Julius Schmänck, 32 years old, cook and baker.
- Tertiary Edmund Wilde, 25 years old, shoemaker, entered the first Order in Teutopolis and was the first novice of the Saxonian Franciscans in North America.
- Tertiary Franz (later Hermann) Uphoff, 37 years old, he administered the group's finances.[33]

The emigrant missionaries adhered to the strict observance and rigor of the Rule. Besides the three priests, the group contained all the skilled craftsmen necessary for an independent friary: a carpenter to construct the buildings, a tailor and shoemaker for the clothes, a gardener, a baker and a cook for food. The tertiaries administered their finances. The Franciscans of the First Order strictly refused to handle money. Nevertheless, they recognized that they needed money and accepted it as alms and contributions.

---

[32] Compare: Willibald Kullmann, „P. Gregor Janknecht," in: *Vita Seraphica* 10 (1929), 52-58, here 54.

[33] See Kilian Schlösser, "Sacred Heart Province Chronicles." 1858-1911, Vol. 1, p. 1-2, SHPA.

The group left Warendorf on August 24 and travelled via Bremen to North America. The Leopold Foundation in Vienna provided for their travel expenses.[34] On October 2, 1858, the Friars officially took charge of the parish in Teutopolis, Illinois. The parish consisted mainly of German immigrants. Teutopolis had been founded in 1839 by immigrants from Oldenburg and Hanover. They had lived without any spiritual care and celebrated their own lay-led church services for many years. To fulfil their Easter duty they had to travel about one hundred miles to St. Louis.[35] Clearly, the Friars had found a parish where they could pursue their zealous missionary ambitions.

However, in order to do so, the Friars had to adopt new rules and institutions. Catholic life in the US differed markedly from what they were accustomed to in Germany. Around 1830 there were only about 150,000 Catholics in the United States consisting of old-stock, wealthy families of English, and Irish and German immigrants. By 1892, the Church consisted of a dizzying array of immigrant groups. According to the *Schematismus der katholischen Geistlichkeit deutscher Zunge in den Vereinigten Staaten Amerikas* there were more than 2,250 Catholic parishes and mission stations in the US.

When they first arrived, many German immigrants found it easier to live in urban centers in order to find work as laborers and crafts-men on railway construction or canal building so that they could earn enough money to purchase their own farms. Unfortunately, there was still a good deal of traditional prejudice against Catholics on the part of many locals, so immigrant Catholics often felt alien-ated from the host culture. What kept them going was their dream of owning their own farm in a community with other German Catholics where they could also have their own church.[36] Many immigrant German farmers hoped that they could improve their lives by moving to America, and felt they could practice their religion more freely in the rural areas. Consequently, about 75 percent of the German Catholics in the US settled in the Midwest.[37] German immi-grants were usually not among the poorest of the poor in their native

---

[34] Joseph Oscar Rauscher to Gregor Janknecht, June 17, 1858, SHPA Safe „Teutopolis. History–Early Friars 1858-1864," Nr. 1.

[35] *Vita Seraphica*, 1929, 50.

[36] Conzen, "German Catholics in America," 575.

[37] Ibid., 574.

country. Many had owned a little land, or had been farm workers, but feared the loss of their social status. Many of them immigrated as whole families. Even before the *Homestead Act* of 1862, Federal land was comparatively cheap. Most immigrants had some money from the sale of their farms in Germany. The difficulties of the subsistence economy in Germany had prepared them for the difficult life on the American frontier. This, then, was the rural scene, which the Franciscans encountered upon their arrival in North America.

As was the case with all the other immigrants, the Franciscans had difficulty finding their way around at first. In the meantime, they encountered various difficulties, surprises and even conflicts with their Rule. P. Servatius Altmicks' letters to Provincial Janknecht from May 1859 give detailed insights into their living conditions in the mission. After their arrival in Teutopolis, the nine Friars of the first mission team lived in a small house with three rooms, which served as both work and bedrooms. Fathers Capistran Zwinge and Servatius Altmicks took over the pastoral care of the surrounding communities. This meant strenuous efforts for the Friars:

> *"We did not only have to give the usual sermons, but often had to hear the confessions of all the believers who came in crowds. The effort that it took to do all this extra work began to tell on us. Before we came here, I had thought it impossible to hear confessions for so many hours a day. But now I can confirm: Omnia possum in eo, qui me confortat. You may imagine that the administration of the sacrament of penance as well as all the other sacraments led to some difficulties. There are cases in which even the most cool-headed moralist would break out into a sweat trying to find a solution to a penitent's problem. But once you get so tired that you think now it can go no further, just then the Lord sends new comfort. This is when such a misled little sheep comes along, who has been wandering around in America's forests for several years and never confessed in this part of the world. Yes, then the joy is certain, and I thank the Lord a thousand times."*[38]

This is a vivid example of how the Franciscans had to adapt their usual ministry to the conditions in America. In the United States, their ministry was determined by the needs of the immigrants. Their main task was to care for the parishes and to fill the schools. In

---

[38] Servatius Altmicks to Gregor Janknecht, Teutopolis May 11, 1859, *Katholisches Missionsblatt* 1860, 5f.

Europe, the Friars were not experienced in pastoral care. Only rarely did they serve as pastors of parishes. Until 1913, a special dispensation from the Rule was necessary before a member of the Order could take over a parish. Even though such a responsibility was not forbidden, it contradicted the spirit of the Rule. As parish priests the Friars were not primarily subordinate to their superior in the Order but to the Bishop. This is the reason why the Friars in Europe and especially those in the Saxonian Province were not prepared to take over these pastoral positions.[39] In Germany, Franciscan ministry was mainly limited to the temporary help and support of secular priests.[40] Besides that, the Saxonian Franciscans looked after places of pilgrimage such as Mount Huelfensberg, organized pilgrimages to these places and conducted missions. The Franciscan Schools in Europe were exclusively for the education of the Friars—they had no establishments for an all-around education. When they were asked in America to educate lay people, this was a new challenge for them. While their life in the Order in Europe had focused internally, they now had to take over more external tasks in America.[41]

In order to fulfil these tasks, the Friars had to apply for various dispensations from the Rule. Thus, Janknecht asked Rome for permission for Friars in America to wear secular clothes outside their friary and to accept money. Altmicks writes:

"Last fall the Americans were quite astonished by our strange appearance. They examined us from head to toe. Then they walked to the Germans to ask them what strange creatures we were. In Teutopolis, some of them thought we were expelled Indians. Nevertheless, they were always nice and friendly and often even benevolent towards us. But one doubt remained among them: We did not accept any money, would not even touch it. This made them doubt that we really had our senses together. In their opinion, we spurned the best. The Americans have almost as much respect for the golden dollar as the

---

[39] Fleckenstein, *Franziskaner*, 163. The General Constitution was revised in 1913. After that special dispensations were no longer required to take over parishes.

[40] Fleckenstein, *Franziskaner*, 169.

[41] Monti, *Friars*, 530. P. Benedikt Mertens describes similar problems of the Tyrolese Friars in adapting the Rules of the Order to the new living conditions in Cincinnati / Ohio and the future Province of John the Baptist. See Benedikt Mertens, "Franciscans and Parochial Ministry. Past and Present Aspects of a Debated Question," in: *Antonianum* LXXV (2000) 523-554, here 534.

Israelites had for the Golden Cow. This prohibition of our Holy Rule, not to accept any money, sometimes leads into difficulties in the mission. We can hardly get along without money when we travel. Either we have to refrain from travelling or we need a special faculty for these cases."[42]

These dispensations were granted without any objection.[43] Nevertheless, the Friars rarely made use of them.[44]

The prohibition to ride horseback was another source of conflict between the Rule and the necessities of life in the New World. Riding in a carriage was prohibited to the Franciscans, since this had been associated with property and riches when the Order was founded. In his letter to Janknecht, Altmicks describes a case where he was called to bring the sacraments to a seriously injured person:

"I went there, put on my riding pants, took the Holy vessels with the Holy oil and went back to the church to get the Holy sacraments. When I came back, the horse was ready, and the two Frenchmen, who had called me, accompanied me. We left the city in a hurry—I do not know where we went. Soon we reached the forest where the passage was difficult. In cases such as this, riding is absolutely necessary. During the day, the roads are difficult to pass—much less at night. Even a good horse has its difficulties to get through. It would be impossible to pass with a coach. By the way, here every female knows how to ride a horse and in doing so is not even conspicuous. Of course, for the sake of our honour, we have to wear dark riding pants under the habit. When we get off the horse, we let down the habit and then the look of the Friar is complete."[45]

These examples demonstrate how difficult it was for the Franciscans to establish their rule in the scattered rural communities. On the one hand they would not have been able to travel far without a horse. On the other hand they knew that the Rule did not permit riding a horse. In his letter Altmicks tries to explain to the Provincial why riding was

---

[42] Servatius Altmicks to Gregor Janknecht, Teutopolis May 11, 1859, *Katholisches Missionsblatt* 1860, 24f.

[43] There is a copy of the dispensation in the Chronicle of the Sacred Heart Province; Schloesser, Chronicles I, 14f.

[44] Schmitz, Cajetan: „Zum Jubilaeum der Ordensprovinz vom Heiligsten Herzen Jesu in Nordamerika," In: *Beitraege zur Geschichte der Saechsischen Franziskanerprovinz vom Heiligen Kreuze I* (1908) 97-112, here 104.

[45] Servatius Altmicks to Gregor Janknecht, Teutopolis May 11, 1859, *Katholisches Missionsblatt* 1860, 30.

necessary for them. Furthermore, horseback riding was ordinary in America and not associated with riches. This shows the problematic nature of transfer. On the one hand the Franciscans brought their Rule and values with them from Europe. However, they partially failed in trying to adapt them to the New World. The long distances between single settlements and poor roads required much more mobility on the part of the Friars than was the case in densely populated Central Europe. As Provincial, Janknecht had always been well-disposed towards the missionaries in America. But the observance of the Rule was at least as important to him.[46] Especially during the first years of the mission, there were numerous conflicts between the Friars in America and their European Superiors concerning the observance of the Rule.[47]

In November 1859 a second group of Friars from the Saxonian Province arrived in America. This group moved into a new friary in Quincy, where the Franciscans were supposed to establish a college.[48] During the following years several small groups of Saxonian Friars arrived to support the North American mission. In addition, there were also locals who joined the Order.

However, the Franciscans were not successful everywhere. Life in the Quincy Friary was quite different from life in Teutopolis. In Quincy, the missionaries were responsible for only a small parish. They did not provide sacramental care for surrounding communities nor did they organize missions. The newly ordained Priest P. Maurice Klostermann wrote to Provincial Maasmann in 1861: "*My work as Priest has been reduced to nearly zero. I read daily Mass with the Friars and sometimes with two or three other people—but sometimes I am alone with the surrounding walls.*"[49]

---

[46] The question of riding and possessing horses recurs several times in Janknecht's letters to the mission. In June 1859 he wrote to the Friars in the American mission: "*Concerning the sick horse, you have to judge its necessity yourself. I am not sure if the horse is the only possibility to get to the sick. At first sight, a need may seem bigger than it eventually turns out to be. Therefore, I regard it as necessary, that you get permission from the Guardian and that you send me a sealed report in important cases.*" Janknecht to the Friars in Teutopolis, June 2, 1859, in SHPA.

[47] Monti, "Franciscan Friars". 530.

[48] Rakemann, Janknecht, 222.

[49] Klostermnn to Maasmann, Quincy December 13, 1861, Archives of the Saxonian Province in Werl (ASFP Werl), Nr. 16.

The day the Franciscans were expelled from Prussia, the mission in America, which had been erected as a Commissariat in 1862, had 124 members who were spread over seven friaries.[50]

3. Refugees of the *Kulturkampf*

The Commissariat grew significantly during the *Kulturkampf*. According to the *Schematismus* of the Holy Cross Province, the correspondence of Gregory Janknecht, passenger lists from the steam boat companies and necrologies of the Holy Cross and later the Sacred Heart Province, the following Friars travelled to North America during the *Kulturkampf*:[51]

Priests:

Name	Birth	Ordination	Year, Place of Death
Isodore Loeser	1823	1849	1875 Teutopolis
Kilian Schloesser ·	1826	1857	1904 St. Barbara
Vincentius Halbfaß	1832	1856	1897 St. Louis
Bonaventura Machuy	1825	1850	1889 Cleveland
Eugenius Puers	1835	1860	1891 Memphis
Damasus Rüsing	1840	1867	1893 Fulda
Pancratius Schulte	1837	1868	1913 Cleveland
Arsenius Fahle	1843	1869	1918 Washington
Markus Thienel	1835	1869	1904 Cleveland
Sebastian Cebulla	1839	1869	1922 Chicago
Michael Richardt	1844	1868	1916 St. Barbara
Guido Knepper	1843	1871	1918 Teutopolis
Clementius Deymann	1844	1872	1896 Phoenix
Maternus Mallmann	1844	1870	1878 Memphis
Anselmus Puetz	1834	1862	1912 Cleveland
Desiderius Liss	1844	1870	*1880 Return*

[50] Rakemann, Janknecht, 224. The friaries were in Teutopolis, Quincy, Cleveland, Memphis and St. Louis. Schmies, Bernd / Rakemann, Kirsten: *Spuren Franziskanischer Geschichte. Chronologischer Abriß der Geschichte der sächsischen Franziskanerprovinzen von ihren Anfängen bis zur Gegenwart.* (Werl, 1999) (Saxonia Franciscana, Special Edition), 491.

[51] See: *Schematismus Provinciae Saxoniae S. Crucis Ordinis FF. Minorum, 1873*, S. 9-21; *Germans to America*, S. 13, 139-140, 146; Janknecht Obödienz, Paderborn June 10, 1875; Janknecht Obödienz, Paderborn July 23, 1875; *Necrology of the Franciscan Province of the Sacred Heart*, Fifth Edition, 1980.

Priests (continued):

Name	Birth	Ordination	Year, Place of Death
Paulus Teroerde	1849	1874	1911 Arkansas
Beda Hansen	1847	1868	*1882 left the Order*
Wolfgang Janietz	1832	1860	*1888 Return*
Martin vom Kolke	1850	1875	*1881 Return*
Eusebius Müller	1850	1875	*1880 Return*
Maximilian Neumann	1846	1875	1934 San Luis
Hilarius Scholz	1848	1875	*1886 Return*
Herbert Mertens	1849	1874	1876 Alton
Mathias Scholly	1847	1875	*1881 Return*
Rufinus Moehle	1847	1874	1914 Minneapolis
Irenäus Bierbaum	1843	1868	*1877 Return*
Ewald Fahle	1848	1873	*1880 Return*
Richardt van Heck	1838	1877	1910 Teutopolis
Casimir Vogt	1845	1869	1919 Los Angeles

Clerics:

Name	Birth	Ordination	Year, Place of Death
Leo Brandys	1857	1877	1887 Radom, Ill.
Clementinus Lorbacher	1848	1873	1887 Quincy
Norbertus Baron	1849	1875	1876 St. Louis
Rufinus Moehle	1847	1874	1914 Minneapolis
Casimirus Hüppe	1849	1875	1914 St. Bernard
Heribertus Mertens	1849	1874	1876 Alton, Ill.
Johannes Gafrcn	1850	1874	1897 Ashland
Eustachius Vollmer	1851	1876	1924 Ashland
Symphorianus Forstmann	1850	1876	1910 Quincy
Suitbertus Albersmann	1851	1878	1909 Jordan, Minn
Aloysius Hoeren	1851	1877	*1881 Return*
Andreas Butzküben	1846	1876	1922 Omaha
Honorius Aremke	1850	1878	1879 Joliet, Ill.
Franciskus Haase	1852	1876	1927 Joliet
Cyprianus Banscheidt	1852	1876	1910 Ashland
Marcellinus Bickmann	1851	1877	1878 St. Louis
Cyrillus Augustinsky	1851	1877	*1887 left the Order*
Engelbertus Gey	1853	1877	1930 San Luis
Benignus Schütz	1852	1878	1925 Qunicy
Laurentius Eppinger	1852	1877	1878 St. Louis
Pacificus Kohnen	1851	1876	1924 Omaha
Quirinius Stücker	1851	1878	1914 S. Francisco
Samuel Macke	1851	1878	1925 Teutopolis

Clerics (continued):

Name	Birth	Ordination	Year, Place of Death
Rochus Boehm	1852	1872	1924 Oshkosh
Henricus Mühlstroh	1854	1872	1877 St. Louis
Paschalis Nolte	1845	1880	1900 Chicago
Jakobus Nolte	1851	1877	1916 St. Barbara
Mauritius Bauckholt	1851	1878	1926 Joliet
Servatius Rasche	1852	1879	1919 Chicago
Stanislaus Kampmann	1855	1879	*1880 Return*
Camillus Wenzel	1830	1874	1909 Cleveland
Josef Sievers	1852	1876	*1897 Return*
Anastasius Czech	1855	1881	1896 Omaha
Odoricus Derenthal	1855	1879	1934 Superior
Leonard Breuer	1856	1876	1876 Teutopolis
Fulgentius Hansen	1850	1878	*1884 left the Order*
Benno Schäfer	1851	1902	*1877 Return*
Dionysius Schroeder	1846	1879	*1880 Return*
Albert Rittner	1851	1879	*1881 Return*
Cornelius Schönwälder	1855	1880	1907 Lake County
Remigius Goette	1856	1880	*1881 Return*
PaulusTolksdorf	1848	1882	1931 Teutopolis
Urban Stanowsky	1856	1880	*1888 left the Order*
Bernard Döbbing	1855	1879	*1881 Return*
Alphons Goette	1857	1881	1908 China
Capistran Goette	1858	1881	1919 China
Damian Kozioleck	1856	1882	1931 Cleveland
Edmund Roediger	1857	1882	1926 Washington
Florentinus Kurzer	1857	1882	1943 Columbus
Hugo Storff	1858	1881	1948 Rome
Nicolaus Stordeur		1874	*1877 left the Order*
Apollinaris Seibert	1858	1884	*1880 Return*
Solano Hilchenbach	1859	1883	1898 Chicago
Oswald Rotter	1852		*1875 left the Order*
Wilhelm Mott	1855	1882	*1882 Return*
Henri Reinkemeyer	1860	1884	1899 Joliet

Lay Brothers:

Name	Birth	Investment	Year, Place of Death
Quirinius Hummels	1820	1847	1879 Teutopolis
Zacharias Broeker	1810	1849	1881 Herrmann
Norbertus Doebbe	1827	1852	1888 Chillicothe
Euphronius Albers	1832	1860	1908 Indianapolis

Lay Brothers (continued):

Name	Birth	Investment	Year, Place of Death
Erasmus Hesse	1836	1860	1878 Memphis
Onesimus Steinmeier	1836	1870	1877 Indianapolis
Servulus Wenning	1846	1872	1943 Washington
Nazarius Schmechta	1835	1858	1886 Radom
Mauritius Kruse	1840	1867	*1880 Return*
Damian Büschgens	1826	1866	1894 Hermann
Diodor Hebbecker	1836	1869	1895 Teutopolis
Hilarius Iven	1833	1870	*1880 Return*
Benignus Pander	1831	1873	1908 St. Louis
Petrus Schurgast	1832	1870	*1881 Return*
Markus Becker	1839	1867	1916 St. Louis
Arnold Wilms	1842	1869	1917 Oakland
Hubert Schneider	1844	1875	1929 St. Louis

Tertiaries:

Name	Birth	Investment	Year, Place of Death
Alphonsus Müller	1840	1868	1914 Jordan, Minn.
Paulinus Stotter	1843	1869	1819 Quincy
Marcus Schaeffer	1841	1871	1905 Indianapolis
Isidorus Tretelski	1845	1872	1922 Quincy
Servulus Wenning	1846	1872	1943 Washington
Wendelin Kummer	1843	1875	1878 Memphis
Dionysius Nacon	1844	1870	1919 Cleveland
Caesar Hünnewinkel			*1880 Return*
Andreas Jacobs		1872	*Left the Order*
Vitali Arnemann	1853	1872	*Left the Order*
Cosimus Orlic	1845	1878	1934 St. Louis

The list shows that the majority of the exiles were Priests and Clerics. The Friars who came to the United States were comparatively young men, only a few older than 40 years of age. The youngest Priest was only 26 years old. Several candidates had not even reached their 20th year. The youngest, Henri Reinkemeyer, was only 14 years old and not even confirmed.[52] Altogether, 114 Franciscans came to the United States in the summer of 1875.

---

[52] This was not unusual in these times. Other Orders also recruited young and inexperienced Priests for their missions in America. Some of these young men had no other opportunities because they either could not afford their education in Germany or did not find an employment. Conzen, German, p. 376f.

The first small group of 18 Friars started to America via Le Havre on February 18, 1875. This group was headed by Servatius Altmicks, who had lived in America since 1858 and had travelled to Germany to discuss organizational issues. They arrived in New York on board the *France* on February 26, 1875.[53] After the proclamation of the *Klostergesetz*, Janknecht sent a telegram to the Friars in Teutopolis: *"Accept five new residences; a great number is coming."*[54]

On June 10, 1875 the first large group of Friars started their journey from Dusseldorf to America. This group consisted of 65 Priests and Brothers, two Tertiaries and 19 candidates.[55] When the Friars boarded their ship at 11 p.m. there was a huge crowd of people present to say farewell to the Franciscans. Various newspapers reported their departure:

> *"It was a touching scene when the Franciscans departed. They had decided to take the evening ship in order to stir as little sensation as possible. The news of their departure had spread through the city like a wildfire. Consequently a big crowd had gathered at the friary, at the harbor and along the shores in order to say a cordial farewell to the departing Friars."*[56]

The reaction of the population was quite remarkable. There were even big crowds when they left their friaries. Where assemblies were forbidden by the police, the faithful decorated their houses with flowers and stood in front of their doors to wave to the departing Friars. This is how they expressed their faithfulness to their shepherds.

> *"77 Friars from Warendorf, Wiedenbruck and Dusseldorf came to the harbor in groups. Among them there were several men who wore the Iron Cross of First or Second Class as a sign of their patriotic attitude. When the honourable men entered the bridge, the believers in the crowd started to sing Catholic songs: a hint that they would keep their Catholic faith even if their shepherds were gone."*[57]

The public display of several patriotic medals by the Franciscans is rather interesting. They demonstrated their loyalty toward a State

---

[53] Glazier / Filby, Germans,13.

[54] Quoted after Schmitz, Jubiläum,107.

[55] Janknecht Obödienz, Paderborn, June 10, 1875 (in SHPA).

[56] *Düsseldorfer Volksblatt*, Nr. 150 from June 11, 1875, p 3.

[57] *Düsseldorfer Volksblatt*, Nr. 150 from June 11, 1875, p 3.

which had forbidden their religious expression and had expelled them because of allegedly hostile activities.

> *"The people were crying and weeping, the Friars' faces displayed their sorrow about the lost fatherland, but all of them were impressed by the active participation of the population. The bells rang and the steamboat 'König' took off with the Friars. Will we see them again? We do not know. But some people may have sworn inwardly to use every constitutional device at elections to bring back these men."*[58]

The article emphasizes the population's unhappiness with the politics of the Prussian government. Bismarck's hostile behaviour against the Church met with a sense of disbelief and anger among the Catholic parts of the population. Consequently many German Catholics hoped that the Franciscans would soon come back.

The second group of refugees from the *Kulturkampf* left Dusseldorf on June 24, 1875. The press also noted their departure. The next morning the *Düsseldorfer Zeitung* wrote:

> *"Yesterday evening about 30 Franciscans left the city on board the steamboat 'König' and moved to America. Most of them come from friaries in Westphalia. Among them was a 17-year-old student of Theology who already wore the habit."*[59]

The young Heribert Mertens was also part of this group. Right after their arrival in the United States he wrote this letter to his parents, a letter full of joy and enthusiasm after the exciting voyage:

> *"We left the friary around 11:30 p.m. There were many faithful Catholics standing on both sides of the gate. They accompanied us with chants and cheers. We left Dusseldorf at 1 a.m. on board of a splendid steamboat. We went down the Rhine till Rotterdam where we arrived on Friday afternoon. Our Reverend P. Definitor, Dutch Franciscans and some gentlemen from Rotterdam welcomed us. At first they led us to a big inn. There we were served marvellous wines. After we had refreshed ourselves, the gentlemen asked us to sing a song. We sang: 'O, Francis, father of the poor' and 'Gentle Queen'. After our chant we were led into the dining-room. I have rarely had such a wonderful meal in my whole life. German and Dutch toasts were given. One Dutch Father said he did not know us and we did*

---

[58] *Düsseldorfer Volksblatt*, Nr. 150 from June 11, 1875, p 3.
[59] *Düsseldorfer Zeitung*, Nr. 149, June 25, 1875.

not know him. But since we are all sons of the same Holy Father, he believed he had to prepare such a reception for us."[60]

This description reads more like a report of a pleasure-trip than of an expulsion by force from a native country and the seeking of refuge in a distant foreign country of exile. Mertens shows no indications of grief or regret about the separation from his family and his native country. It is much more the letter of a young man, hungry for adventure. He mixes his youthful enthusiasm with the Franciscan ability to subsist on very little under difficult circumstances.

"After dinner the gentlemen accompanied us to the ship, which would bring us to the New World. After we had inspected the ship, they offered to show us the splendid city of Rotterdam. I can hardly describe the impression which the city made upon us with all its huge ships and magnificent buildings. That is how the first day came to an end. But the joy of the day was still to continue: Around 7 p.m. Dr. Koenaart led us into his apartment. Dear parents, you should have seen this Dutch house. All rooms and staircases from basement to the roof were covered with the most expensive carpets. The doctor's family was already prepared for our visit and received us as warmly and gently as I have rarely experienced before. For us Germans, it was strange when we heard the gentle ladies speaking Dutch. It was as if we were talking to a Westphalian peasant woman. After we had been together for quite a while, the whole family brought us back to our ship, where we would spend the night. At 7 in the morning the big steam boat put to sea."[61]

Not all Friars were so happy about their journey to America. Several of them would have preferred to stay in their German friaries—as their letters from the United States prove. On June 20, 1875, Gregory Janknecht wrote from Vienna to the Minister General in Rome: *"All Clerics, some Priests and Brothers have set off for America, altogether 100."*[62]

---

[60] Heribert Mertens to his parents, St. Louis July 19, 1875 (Henniges, Diodor: Briefe aus der Kulturkampfzeit. In: *Vita Seraphica* 8 [1927] 26-29, here 26f.).

[61] Heribert Mertens to his parents, St. Louis July 19, 1875 (Henniges, Briefe, 26f.). Many immigrants described the food, drinks and clothes in great detail when they wrote to their relatives back in Germany. They compared everything with their experiences in Germany. The descriptions were supposed to demonstrate their social rise. Helbich, Wolfgang: *Briefe aus Amerika. Deutsche Auswanderer schreiben aus der Neuen Welt, 1830-1930* (München, 1988), 34.

[62] Janknecht to General Minister, July 20, 1875 (Reinhold, Korrespondenz, 56).

From Dusselforf they travelled to Rotterdam by steam boat, where they boarded the ocean liner. The second group of Friars left Europe on June 12 on board the *SS Rotterdam*. Their ocean journey took two weeks, which passed boringly and uneventfully. It rained almost every day and was mostly foggy. Captain Jansen permitted the Franciscans to use one room as a chapel. An altar was erected so the Friars could celebrate Mass and fulfil their religious duties. Shortly before Newfoundland the *SS Rotterdam* almost hit a fishing boat in the fog.[63]

On June 30 the exiles arrived in New York. They were welcomed in the harbour by local Franciscans. They spent the night in the local friary or in private houses. The next day, 76 friars took a train to Teutopolis. The remaining nine Friars had mistakenly been brought to the wrong station and missed the train. The Erie Railway Company had added an extra car for the Friars. However, there was hardly enough space for 76 men to sit in it, much less to recline. The journey took another two days and two nights. Besides that, the Franciscans had no money with them. Their treasurer, William Kirchfeldt (the only candidate in the group), was one of the group who had missed the train in New York.[64] On July 4, 1875, the starving Friars eventually reached their final destination of Teutopolis after 26 days en route.[65] The other group under the leadership of P. Vinzentius Halbfaß took the same route and arrived in Teutopolis on July 14, 1875.[66]

The following year two smaller groups of exiles from the Saxonian Province arrived in the United States. The first one consisted of three Priests, two Clerics and two Brothers. They arrived in Teutopolis on September 11, 1876. The second group was accompanied by Provincial Gregory Janknecht and arrived in October of 1876. It consisted of two Priests, one Brother and two Candidates.[67] The number

---

[63] Eugene Hagedorn, "History of St. Francis Monastery, Teutopolis, Illinois," in *Teutopolis Press*, March 11, 1909.

[64] Since the Friars of the First Order were not allowed to carry money, they entrusted their travel money to the members of the Third Order or to the candidates, who had not yet entered the First Order. This is also how the Franciscans handled money on a daily basis: Either Tertiaries or 'spiritual friends' collected money and alms for them.

[65] Anselm Puetz, *Annals of the Franciscan Province of the Sacred Heart*, Nr. 8, St. Louis, 1932, 530-542.

[66] Habig, *Heralds*, 108-113.

[67] Habig, *Heralds*, 113.

of Friars in the Commissariat more than doubled during the *Kulturkampf*.[68] However, this created various new problems.

In Teutopolis the new arrivals were put up in the Friary and in the College since the students were on vacation. However, the building in Teutopolis was far too small to accommodate such a large number of Friars. This unexpected growth made the establishment of new houses necessary. Therefore, Commissary P. Mauritius Klostermann called together the Discretorium in St. Louis right after the arrival of the exiles. They decided to take over St. Peter's in Chicago and six other missions in Jordan, Minnesota. In addition the Franciscans bought land in Indianapolis to erect a new friary, and another House was established in Hermann, Missouri. The Friary in Teutopolis was enlarged for the 60 Friars who remained there. Additional cells were established in the attic. The same thing took place in St. Louis. In Quincy, a third floor was added to the building.[69] Between 1875 and 1879 ten new friaries were officially opened and four others were close to being established as friaries: St. Joseph's Friary and College in Cleveland; St. Mary's Friary in Memphis; St. George's Friary in Hermann, Missouri; Sacred Heart Friary in Indianapolis, St. Peter's Friary in Chicago; St. John the Baptist Friary in Jordan, Minnesota; St. John the Baptist Friary in Joliet, Illinois; St. Mary of the Angels Friary in Wien, Missouri; St. Bonaventure Friary in Columbus, Nebraska; St. Columban Friary in Chillicothe, Missouri; Holy Family Friary in Bayfield, Wisconsin; Guardian Angel Friary in Chaska, Minnesota; St. Martin of Tours Friary in Rhineland, Missouri; St. Michael Friary in Radom, Illinois and St. Bernard Friary in Lindsay, Nebraska.[70] In addition the Franciscans took over parochial tasks in numerous cities and surrounding villages in order to meet the need for German-speaking Priests among the German Catholics.

In 1873 Janknecht had granted Commissary P. Mauritius Klostermann several powers of attorney concerning the North American Commissariat, having foreseen the coming persecution. Nevertheless, Klostermann still needed the Provincial's and the

---

[68] According to the Schematism of the Saxonian Province of the Holy Cross, there were 99 Friars in American Friaries and Houses by 1873. *Schematismus Provinciae Saxoniae S. Crucis Ordinis FF. Minorum* 1873, 17-21.

[69] Schloesser, Chronicles I 63.

[70] See Habig, *Heralds,* 131-151.

Definitorium's consent for appointments and the transfer of Friars from one friary to another. This made it difficult to react quickly and simply to the flood of refugees of the *Kulturkampf*. Many houses were too crowded. The establishment of new foundations needed the Provincial's consent. The Superiors often kept their offices for more than the regular term of three years. Because of the long postal delay, Janknecht authorized the Commissary to directly contact the Minister General in Rome. The Commissary was asked to send a report to the Saxonian Provincial only every quarter of the year.[71] This degree of independence was attributed to the *Kulturkampf* and the difficulties of communication.

On February 17, 1876, Commissary Klostermann first made use of the privilege. In a letter to the General he described the conditions in the Commissariat and asked for permission to establish new houses and to convert existing houses into friaries. Klostermann also proposed to hold a Provincial Chapter under the leadership of P. Vincenz Halbfaß, in order to make the necessary decisions and to grant dispensations.[72] Again, due to the long postal delays, Klostermann did not know at this time that Janknecht had confirmed all current Superiors in December 1875. Furthermore, he had negotiated with the Minister General the separation of the Commissariat from the Mother Province. Janknecht was quite aware that an independent American Province had many advantages for the Friars living there. On the other hand, he wanted to maintain his influence on the Commissariat during the *Kulturkampf*. In his letter to the General he writes:

"I could hardly do anything against the unanimous consent of the Commissary and his Discretes. When the Patres intended the separation of their mission one year ago, I had already contacted you. In accordance with the Definitorium, I only opposed the separation because of the coming suppression. This fear was not unfounded as it later turned out. If the Commissariat had been separated from our persecuted Province, we would have had to humbly ask for accommodation. Instead, I could freely send Friars to America, for the benefit of the Province and of the individual. Next January, I will send even more Friars to America. Thus, the Mission is independent from the Province. But the Mother Province can still intervene if necessary."[73]

---

[71] Janknecht to General December 28, 1875, *Vita Seraphica* 29, 60.
[72] Habig, *Heralds*, 165.
[73] Janknecht to General December 28, 1875, *Vita Seraphica* 29,60.

It is clear that the Commissariat had already asked for separation as an independent Province even before the arrival of the exiles. Being an independent Province made local administration much easier than having to go through Europe. Janknecht had refused this plea because of the possible effects of the *Kulturkampf*. In the end, this allowed him to send large numbers of Friars to the American Commissariat. But even after the successful accommodation of refugees, he still wanted to keep his control over the Commissariat. In case the Province regained its friaries in Prussia, he wanted to be able to call back the Friars. He wanted to make this right a prerequisite for the independence of the American Province.[74] Obviously, Janknecht had not given up hope for a swift end to the *Kulturkampf*. On the other hand, the extensive renovations at the Dutch and Belgian Friaries reflect the long-term planning of the exile.[75]

An independent American Province posed another problem to the Saxonian Provincial: According to the Rule, the members of a Commissariat had the option to return to their Mother Province before the Commissariat was erected as a Province.[76] If a great number of Friars wished to remain with the Mother Province, new logistical difficulties would have been created for Janknecht. He would have had to find more space in the already overcrowded friaries in Holland and Belgium.

But Janknecht was not generally opposed to an independent American Province. In the end, it was the Minister General in Rome who rejected the Commissariat's request for separation from the Saxonian Province. Due to the political turmoil, the General also delayed Janknecht's visitation of the Commissariat. Only when Klostermann urged him not to postpone his visitation anymore did Janknecht start out on his third journey to America.[77]

During his stay of 16 months, Janknecht inspected new houses, visited old friaries and appointed new Guardians. The goal of his trip was to place the Commissariat on solid ground and to prepare for its even-

---

[74] *"This should be a prerequisite, that the Province could call back all the Friars, when it gets back its original friaries."* See Janknecht to General December 28, 1875, *Vita Seraphica* 29, 60.

[75] Rakemann, Janknecht, 236.

[76] Schmitz, Jubiläum, 109.

[77] Habig, *Heralds*, 167-170.

tual separation from the Mother Province. In his farewell letter before his return to Holland Janknecht wrote: *"I go back to Europe in order to achieve the independence of the American Mission as a Province."*[78] After consultations with the Provincial Definitorium in Holland and the Minister General in Rome, Janknecht sent a circular letter to the friars in the American Commissariat. In this letter from November 27, 1878, he informed them that the Definitorium of the Saxonian Province and the Minister General in Rome have agreed to the erection of the American Commissariat as an independent Province. All the friars had the choice to stay in the new Province or to return to their original Province—in this case to the Dutch or Belgian exile. They had to respond within three days of receiving the letter.[79]

On March 16, 1879, Pope Leo XIII authorized the Minister General and the General Definitorium to proceed with the canonical erection of the American Province. On April 26, 1879, the General Definitorium decided that the North American Commissariat would become the Sacred Heart Province.[80] Vincenz Halbfaß became the first Provincial Minister. At the same time, the General Definitorium relieved Janknecht of his office and appointed Othmar Maasmann as new Provincial of the Saxonian Province. Janknecht had repeatedly asked to be replaced during the previous years. The difficult political circumstances, the persecution by German authorities, the administration of a divided Province as well as the strenuous journeys over long distances had made him sick of office after 18 years.[81] Before his return to Europe Janknecht had written to the Minister General in 1877:

"At this occasion I will not conceal that it is my earnest decision to resign from office after I return to Holland. It is impossible for me to continue. I want to be released from the sorrows and difficulties of such an extensive administrative task."[82]

Furthermore, Janknecht was plagued by doubts about himself. He had repeatedly asked the General to forgive him his numerous mis-

---

[78] Gregor Janknecht to Klostermann, Jersey City, March 9, 1878, "Provincials' Letters to American Missions. 1859-1878," Nr. 77, SHPA.

[79] Gregor Janknecht, "Circular Letters. Provincial / General. 1859-1913," SHPA.

[80] Habig, *Heralds*, 172f.

[81] Rakemann, Janknecht, 236-239.

[82] Janknecht to General, December 22, 1877, *Vita Seraphica* 29, 69-70.

takes, carelessness and imperfections.[83] This finally resulted in a serious mental illness. Janknecht regularly experienced feelings of anxiety and apprehension during public appearances and speeches. In the end he could not even offer grace at meals anymore and the Provincial had to release him from all official duties within the Province for quite a while.[84]

During the years following the separation, the young American Province spread even further. Shortly after its erection as a Province, the leadership moved to St. Louis which was much more centrally located than Teutopolis and was becoming a major city. St. Anthony Friary became the headquarters of the Province. In 1886 the young Province was asked to take over a convent in California.[85] It was the old Santa Barbara Mission founded in 1786 during the California mission era. The house was on the verge of extinction. With the influx of personnel from the Sacred Heart Province, the Mission flourished again. In addition, eight more houses were taken over in California and Arizona during the next twenty years, among them friaries in San Francisco, Los Angeles and Sacramento. Other residences followed and in 1915 the friaries in California and Arizona were combined into the independent St. Barbara Province.[86]

During their first decades the American Friars devoted themselves mainly to the pastoral care of German immigrants. After the separation from the Saxonian Province, some Friars turned their attention to the mission among the Native Americans. One of them was Servatius Altmicks. The Franciscans ministered among the Chippewa, the Menominee and the Ottawa living in Wisconsin and Michigan.[87]

4. Life in the New World Between Adaptation and Defense

Up to this point we have focused on the emigration of the exiles and the establishment of a new province in the United States. Let us now turn to the personal experiences of the friars by examining the

---

[83] Janknecht to General, April 5, 1878, *Vita Seraphica* 29, 70.

[84] Maasmann to General June 3, 1881, *Vita Seraphica* 29, 80-81, Also Rakemann, Janknecht, 241f.

[85] Schmitz, Jubiläum, 111.

[86] Habig, *Heralds*, 248.

[87] Schmitz, Jubiläum, 106.

letters and memoirs from some of the Friars who went to America during the *Kulturkampf*, which depict their experiences during the first years in the American mission. For instance take P. Anselm Puetz. His report allows an in-depth insight into Franciscan life on the American Frontier. He did not find anything that he had taken for granted in Europe. There were neither solid churches nor regular food. Parochial ministry took place over long distances which had to be travelled by exhausting means of transport. At first he was responsible for the church in Green Creek, about seven miles from Teutopolis. Every week he travelled from Teutopolis to Green Creek on difficult routes through the forest. The church consisted of 50 or 60 families. They had come to America in the 1840s and also had their roots in Hanover and Oldenburg as did the people in Teutopolis. Puetz describes them as solid, unsophisticated, weather-resistant and extremely German people. They had arduously extracted their barren living from the soil. Even though they were consumed by gruelling labor, these sober and hard-working settlers had surprisingly not forgotten about their religious needs. During the first years they had to make their way through the forest with axes and hatchets in order to go to church in Teutopolis. Later, they obtained their own priest and built a log church. Apparently, their spiritual condition was rather solid. Puetz writes:

> *"Pastoring among these good people was not difficult. I went there every Friday afternoon and read Mass. On Saturdays I taught catechism to the children. On Sunday mornings I heard confessions and distributed the Holy Communion. At 10 a.m. was high Mass and sermon. In the afternoon was Sunday school, devotions and blessings. On Mondays I taught in the morning and around 4 p.m. I returned to the Friary in Teutopolis."*[88]

In his memoirs Puetz also describes the primitive living conditions of the settlers and the poor or non-existent roads. However, he liked his ministry among the German settlers in Green Creek; they did not make demands of him beyond his strengths.

However, this soon changed. In January 1878 he was transferred to the northwest frontier, to Columbus, Nebraska, together with P.

---

[88] „Erinnerungen vom Hochw. P. Anselm Puetz (O.F.M.)," in *Manuscripts*, Eugene Hagedorn, S. 3, SHPA.

Ambrosius Jannsen as Praeses. Nebraska had only been settled recently. However, it had become home for many immigrants. The removal of the Native Americans, new railways and free farm land attracted large numbers of immigrants. Entire German or Eastern European villages moved there.[89] According to Puetz, there was a severe lack of priests in the large Vicariate, which reached from Missouri to Nebraska, Wyoming, and Montana and as far as Salt Lake City. Upon their arrival in Omaha, the two Friars were welcomed by the local Bishop:

"The Reverend Bishop welcomed us warmly. He was visibly happy. He gave us all faculties. He endowed us with the pastoral care of Columbus, Platte County, as our headquarters and all neighboring counties: Madison in the North, Polk in the South, Buttler in the Southeast. There are also Germans on the other side of the river. He asked us to found new churches wherever we think it is good. Moreover, he asked us to assist the Irish settlements which were left without pastoral care. Thus, we were determined to work as pioneers."[90]

This was a fairly demanding task for two men. Puetz at first stayed in Omaha and took over the local parish work, while Jannsen went to Columbus. The care for such a large territory obviously led to several problems:

"Now our missionary work began. The news that there was a German Priest in Columbus quickly spread and we received calls for help from within and without the County. We helped as well as we could. P. Ambros had to travel a lot. Travelling was exhausting: The only railway went from East to West. Besides that we used the farm wagon or the U.S. Mail Coach for our journeys."[91]

The means of transportation were not all that was primitive. The existing churches consisted mostly of nailed boards and offered little protection against wind and rain. In his memoirs Puetz describes, how he was called to Battle Creek one day:

"I had to bring everything necessary for Mass: vestments, altar stone, Mass book, prayer book, candlestick, cross and wine. The people in Battle Creek

---

[89] Paul S. Boyer, *The Enduring Vision: A History of the American People* (Lexington, 1995),370.

[90] Hagedorn, Erinnerungen, 5.

[91] Hagedorn, Erinnerungen, 6.

had a church, but what kind of a church?! A raw wooden building, raw boards served as benches, a red mosquito net was the baldachino, the confessional had no grille. I had everything necessary in my trunk. But wherever I came, I had to celebrate Mass in the most wretched places, especially in Madison County."[92]

Solid churches were as uncommon as regular food for the Franciscans. They were neither allowed nor willing to bring money with them. A Provincial Administration that would take care of the nutrition of the Friars did not exist in these times. Thus, the Friars depended upon alms and invitations from the people. However, this practice was not popular everywhere. The following account describes Puetz's attempt to collect alms in an Austrian settlement:

"These Austrians could not understand, that a priest would beg. One of the farmers offered to drive me around, but he was too poor to give something. They all welcomed me in a friendly and respectful way, but nobody gave anything. In the end I received 13 onions. Instead of a car full of wheat, ham, butter and eggs, I brought home 13 onions for dinner."[93]

This scarcity stood in marked contrast to regular and generous meals they were used to in their Mother Province.[94] The Austrians, however, were not used to supporting the priest or church. In Austria, everything was already generously paid for by the state. Later, they came to understand that the Franciscans depended upon their support and they gave freely. Despite the poor living conditions Puetz usually took the circumstances with Franciscan calmness and a certain amount of humor.

Another insight into Franciscan ministry is found in Heribert Mertens' letters to his parents. From the time of his arrival in America Mertens lived in the Friary in Teutopolis and drew a happy picture of his work:

"Here in America we have many possibilities to work for the salvation of souls. There is still a need for priests. Some places have been without pastoral care for a long time and the effects are clearly visible when you get

[92] Hagedorn, Erinnerungen, 7.
[93] Hagedorn, Erinnerungen, 8.
[94] See the chapter about meals in Fleckenstein, Franziskaner, 142-146.

there. Thirteen-year-old children did not even know the Apostle's Creed and I had to lay it into their mouth word for word. I feel sorry for these poor children. It is a burden that they even come. Thus, the priest has to be especially tender and loving with them."[95]

As a newly ordained priest, Mertens could hardly wait to practice his profession among the faithful:

"After the Holy Mass I was called to a sick woman. Because of her Protestant husband she had not been to confession for 17 years. I found her well prepared and gave her new heart. Since I was not yet allowed to hear confessions, I promised to send another priest as soon as possible. It did not take long before he came. The poor sinner confessed and is already in Heaven by now."[96]

Again and again Mertens expresses his belief that God is well-disposed towards their work and that he would reward their *"sacrifice of obedience."*[97] In the spirit of St. Francis he denies himself and makes himself the servant of his environment. He willingly accepts any kind of difficulty.

Every friar reacted to his experience in the New World differently, depending on his personality and individual expectations. For some, life in exile meant fulfilment and the joy of having found a new responsibility. For others it was pure adventure. But there were also Friars who could not accept their new life. The letters of some of these Franciscans display a sense of disappointment in light of the difficult living conditions and the unfamiliar environment. One of these Friars was Hermann (Johannes) Wirtz. He came to America in 1861 and fought in the Civil War. After that his life proceeded in a more peaceful direction. In 1868 he was invested as a Franciscan. He studied at Quincy and Teutopolis and after 1874 he became a professor himself. He received two warnings for violating the Rule.[98] In 1877 he wrote several letters to Janknecht, asking for his release.

"I have received your dear letter from August 13. Reading it, I was convinced that it stemmed from a heart full of brotherly love. Thus the more I

---

[95] Heribert Mertens to his parents, St. Louis Febr. 2, 1876 (in: Henniges, Briefe, 27).

[96] Heribert Mertens to his parents, St. Louis Febr. 2, 1876 (in: Henniges, Briefe, 27).

[97] Heribert Mertens to his parents, St. Louis Febr. 2, 1876 (in: Henniges, Briefe, 28).

[98] Personal file Herman Wirtz in SHPA.

am saddened to request for my release from the Order and for my secular-
ization, because I do not find happiness in the Order anymore. It is the pro-
fessorship which makes it impossible for me to stay. My aversion to it is
continuously growing. Despite this aversion I believe I have been faithful to
all my duties."

Wirtz had accepted the teaching post at Teutopolis against his better
judgment. His aversion to teaching grew over the years. He was not
alone in this feeling. Most of the immigrant Friars showed little
interest in teaching, especially since this had not been part of their
duties in Europe.[99] Janknecht did not grant Wirtz's request to be
transferred to another friary. Thus Wirtz had concluded that he had
to leave the Order.

"I have given up my original plan to enter the military as soon as possible.
Instead, I have decided to return to Germany and look for a job. In
America it would be difficult for me to work as a secular priest or to enter
another Order."[100]

Apparently, Wirtz had decided to take drastic measures in order to
leave the Order. In a second letter to Janknecht a few days later he
sounds more calm. However, his dissatisfaction about his life and his
wish for change is still explicit. Moreover he emphasizes his home-
sickness and longing for relatives:

"Originally I had planned to make one last attempt to remain in the Order.
But now I beg you to take the steps necessary for my secularization. I am
not certain if I will feel better outside the Order. But I hope so. Recently, I
feel the impact of an irresistible longing for Germany and my family. This
may contribute to my unease in the Order."[101]

In 1878 Wirtz volunteered to serve during the Yellow Fever epidemic in Memphis. From there he was called back and sent to Italy.
Later, he returned to the US and died in California in 1905. But he
never was released from the Order. Wirtz may have been an extreme

[99] *Annals of the Franciscan Province of the Sacred Heart*, Vol. 9 (St. Louis, 1933),
570.

[100] Hermann Wirtz to Gregory Janknecht, Teutopolis May 4, 1877, ASFP Werl.

[101] Hermann Wirtz to Gregory Janknecht, Teutopolis May 15, 1877, ASFP Werl.

case, but there were also Friars who left the Order in Germany. However, many other Friars besides Wirtz suffered from American living conditions and from their distance from homeland. One indication of this is the great number of Friars who later returned to Germany after the *Kulturkampf*. But even experienced missionaries had difficulties in the American Commissariat and wished to go back to Germany (see later the example of Lucius Buchholz).

It was not only the difficult living conditions on the Frontier that made life difficult for the Friars, but also the new social and religious surroundings and various personal disappointments. The natural conditions such as climate and unusual diseases posed threats to the refugees of the *Kulturkampf*. Some of them died shortly after their arrival in America. When they arrived in Teutopolis, the Friars had to get used to extreme heat. The summers are extremely hot and humid. Death from excessive heat was not unusual. Equally troubling were the severe winters.

Father Isidorus Loeser died shortly after his arrival in Teutopolis at the age of 50. The strains of the trip and the unfamiliar climate had weakened his body too much. He died on October 8, 1875. His necrology reads:

> *"The exertions of the journey and the unwanted climate proved too severe for the frail constitution of Father Isidore. After the long and dangerous voyage he at once joyfully began life in our convent but he soon contracted a serious sickness. Three months had hardly elapsed after his arrival when his death, precious in the sight of the Lord, brought him to his true fatherland. With great patience and joyfulness he endured his lingering infirmities and the acute pains of his final sickness."*[102]

Another cause for lament was the death of the young Heribert Mertens at the age of 27. As described above, he had come to America eager to work as a priest. Mertens' story is recounted in a letter from his teacher Servatius Altmicks to his parents. The newly ordained priest was supposed to help out in Alton from August 13-20. A few days earlier, he had caught a cold during a sick call. When he arrived in Alton he already felt unwell. He could not attend dinner and went to bed early. The Parish Priest Peters reported:

---

[102] Obituary of Fr. Isidore Loeser, in SHPA.

"At a quarter past two, I heard an enormous cry. The people downstairs said he had talked for half an hour. They had assumed he was praying. When I came to him, he lay in convulsions. I called for Father Janssen (Vicar General of Alton) and the doctor. The doctor explained he would die. Thus, we gave him absolution, Extreme Unction and the last rites. He quietly died while we prayed for him. He never regained consciousness again."[103]

The 25-year-old Leonard Breuer also died in October of 1876. He became sick in St. Louis from typhoid fever on October 10, 1876 and died within two days. Norbert Baron died just as unexpectedly from tuberculosis on Christmas Day 1876 at the age of 27.[104] The deaths of these men illustrate that life in America brought sudden and unexpected dangers. To be sure, death and severe disease were not limited to the Franciscans. All immigrants had to cope with these dangers.

The same is true for Yellow Fever. Europeans experienced devastating epidemics during settlement. The disease started with sudden rheumatic pains, anxiety, high fever, black vomit and in many cases resulted in yellow skin. Those infected usually died within a few days. This made the disease much more threatening than other epidemics such as tuberculosis, typhoid or smallpox, which caused numerous deaths as well. Fear of Yellow Fever was widespread in the South. The first indication of the disease often created mass panic: Its appearance would stop the entire public life of a city. When a city became infected, the epidemic usually lasted an entire summer until the first frost in the fall. Low temperatures killed the tropic pathogen. In 1853 half of all deaths in New Orleans were caused by the Yellow Fever epidemic. The biggest epidemics took place in Norfolk, Virginia with 2,807 deaths in 1855, and in Memphis with 2,000 deaths in 1873 and 5,000 more in 1878.[105] It took until the 1930s for a cure to be found and for hygiene to become advanced enough to protect from Yellow Fever. The means of infection had long been unknown. In 1900 Walter Reed found out that the pathogen was transmitted by infected mosquitoes. Armed with this knowledge,

---

[103] Servatius Altmicks to Heribert Mertens' parents (Henniges, Briefe, 29).

[104] See *Annals of the Franciscan Province of the Sacred Heart*, Vol. 1, Nr. 2, St. Louis 1929, 89-92.

[105] Margaret Humphreys, *Yellow Fever and the South* (New Brunswick, 1992), 1-5.

people started to destroy the mosquitoes' breeding-grounds and thus to annihilate the insects.[106]

In 1878 some of the Friar-exiles got a taste of the dangers of Yellow Fever. When the disease broke out in Memphis in the summer of 1878, following two previous epidemics in 1873 and 1875, about 25,000 inhabitants fled the city. Of the remaining 19,000 inhabitants, 17,000 caught the Fever and 5,000 died.[107] At this time Father Lucius Buchholz was Parish Priest and Guardian of the local friary in Memphis. He lived there together with P. Aloysius Wiewer, Br. Amandus Jung and three exiles P. Maternus Mallmann, Br. Erasmus Hesse and Br. Wendelin Kummer. Four Saxonian Franciscans died during the course of the epidemic. The first was Br. Erasmus Hesse. He died on August 31, 1878. The next was Br. Amandus Jung. He had been transferred to Cleveland after the first epidemic. But when the second epidemic started, he asked to return to Memphis. He and the Superiors believed he was immune to Yellow Fever. This, however, proved to be a fatal mistake. Because of his work among the sick, he contracted the disease and died on September 5, 1878. When the Franciscan Sisters of the Third Order happened to visit the friary, they found all the Friars sick. Despite the Friars' rules of enclosure, the Sisters decided to stay in the friary. They buried the dead and nursed the others during their last days.[108] P. Maternus Mallmann's letters to the Commissary Mauritius Klostermann give insight to what was happening in Memphis. In his letter dated August 15, 1878, Mallmann still sounds optimistic:

> *"The Yellow Fever is rapidly increasing. There are many sick calls. Yesterday, I had at least 400 confessions and five sick calls. Pray for us and let other Friars pray for us. I feel a little sick, but I persevere. I do not think it is dangerous for me to stay here, for I have been sick just recently."*[109]

[106] William Coleman, *Yellow Fever in the North: The Methods of Early Epidemiology* (Madison, 1987), 5-11.

[107] Leo Kalmer (O.F.M.), "Stronger than Death: Historical Notes on the Heroic Sacrifices of Catholic Priests and Religious during the Yellow Fever Epidemics at Memphis in 1873, 1878 and 1879" (Memphis, 1929), 7.

[108] Habig, *Heralds*, 155-157.

[109] Maternus Mallmann to Mauritius Klostermann, Memphis, August 15, 1878, "Letters of Memphis. 1878-1888," Nr. 1b, SHPA.

The next letter, which was dated August 16, sounds more dramatic:

"The Yellow Fever has become extremely devastating. Yesterday, I gave the last rites to nine people. They will all die on the third or fourth day. Luckily, between 20,000 and 30,000 people have left the city already. There is a horrible frenzy. There are no tearless faces anymore. Yesterday, I attended to a teacher's eldest son. Today he will die himself and his wife is sick as well. Moreover, I attended to a woman and baptized her dying child, while her husband's and son's dead bodies were brought out of the same room and the bedclothes were burned."[110]

Mallmann's last letter is full of despair and the feeling of abandonment:

"Why do you leave me without any answer? The Fever is spreading awfully. Everybody is dying. The teacher's eldest son died yesterday at 6 p.m. His wife will die tomorrow. Fortunately the city is almost empty. Entire streets and districts are completely deserted. Everybody is gone."[111]

Despite his best efforts, Mallmann caught Yellow Fever and died on September 9, 1878 at the age of 34. In the meantime many Sisters also caught the Fever. They all died between September 10 and 12. The last one was Wendelin Kummer, who succumbed to the Yellow Fever on October 15, 1878.[112] The following summer the Yellow Fever broke out again in Memphis. This time P. Chrysostomus Beineke died. After his death the Friars noticed the inflamed soles of his feet. During his many priestly ministrations he had literally walked them raw. Buchholz then wrote to the current Provincial P. Vincenz Halbfaß:

"P. Chrysostomus died yesterday at 11.40 a.m. He was caught by the fever at nine a.m. It was so intense that he felt as if he were burning. There was no chance to save his life."[113]

The Yellow Fever epidemic and Maternus Mallmann's letters allow still another insight into Franciscan life. Things were not always har-

---

[110] Maternus Mallmann to Mauritius Klostermann, Memphis, August 16, 1878, "Letters of Memphis. 1878-1888," Nr. 1c, SHPA.

[111] Maternus Mallmann to Mauritius Klostermann, Memphis, August 17, 1878, "Letters of Memphis. 1878-1888," Nr. 1d, SHPA.

[112] Habig, *Heralds*, 157f.

[113] Buchholz to Halbfaß, Memphis, September 10, 1879 (SHPA).

monious among the Friars. The previously mentioned Hermann Wirtz had volunteered for service among the sick in Memphis. However, it seems that he could not cope with the mental distress and suffering during the epidemic and turned to alcohol for relief. In his letter to the Commissary, Mallmann writes on August 14:

"P. Hermann is stoned from morning till evening. What is he good for? If we could only get rid of him! Stop Hermann. Pray for us, otherwise we will all die from anger."[114]

This was not all. The situation obviously got worse during the next days:

"Yesterday evening P. Hermann returned home blind drunk. He could not even stand straight anymore. He shouted: 'All Franciscans shall go to hell and see the devil.' When he met Father Hesse, he told him that he [Hesse] is the biggest swine in the world."[115]

Mallmann's plea to recall Hermann Wirtz remained as unanswered as his plea for support in the struggle against the Yellow Fever. In his third letter he threatened to take actions against Wirtz himself:

"P. Hermann left the house yesterday morning at six with two bottles of communion wine. He had neither attended Mass nor prayed. I have no idea where the two bottles are. But I am certain that Hermann drank from morning till evening. Late at night I sent a Brother to look for him. He found him and brought him home blind drunk. Hermann is such a source of offense that I feel forced to make it public in the newspaper that he is no longer one of us if you will not call him back within a few days."[116]

This sad example suggests that not all Friars got along so easily in the New World. The Friars had to fight the same weaknesses and temptations as the people outside the Order. Unfortunately, this aspect has been fully excluded from Franciscan historiography. Neither the rel-

---

[114] Maternus Mallmann to Mauritius Klostermann, Memphis, August 14, 1878, "Letters of Memphis. 1878-1888," Nr. 1a, SHPA.

[115] Maternus Mallmann to Mauritius Klostermann, Memphis, August 15, 1878, "Letters of Memphis. 1878-1888," Nr. 1b, SHPA.

[116] Maternus Mallmann to Mauritius Klostermann, Memphis, August 16, 1878, "Letters of Memphis. 1878-1888," Nr. 1c, SHPA.

evant literature about the Yellow Fever epidemic nor history books about the Franciscans in the U.S. mention such cases. And in the translations and copies of Mallmann's letters the passages quoted above are omitted and marked with ". . .".

Another disappointed Franciscan was P. Lucius Buchholz, the former Guardian of the friary in Memphis. According to Mallmann's letters, Buchholz left when the epidemic broke out: *"There is no hint of Lucius."*[117] Indeed, there are no entries about Lucius Buchholz in the parish book between September 15 and December 21, 1878. The parish book usually keeps a record of all activities in the parish. There are other Friars mentioned in the book in connection with baptisms and funerals during this time.[118] Later history books referred to Buchholz as a dishonourable traitor. In 1897 D. A. Quinn wrote in the *Catholic News*:

> *"Amongst the runaways were several prominent city officials. Two priests left Memphis whilst fever prevailed. Rev. Father Bokel, O.P., having lost his young nephew, a priest, by fever in 1878, was called away from the city by his Superior. The other priest was pastor of St. Mary's German Church, Rev. Father Lucius Buchholz, O.S.F."*[119]

Buchholz' own letters, however, convey a totally different impression. Soon after the epidemic broke out he wrote to the German Provincial, Gregory Janknecht, and introduced his letter full of resignation and grief:

> *"I had intended to write you for a long time in order to explain to you truthfully the events of the past three months. Today, I received the sad news of your resignation and that it was accepted by the Reverend General. Now I could not wait any longer. What a strong blow your resignation is for all of us, but twice as much for me, who had to endure so much bitterness over the last three months. It is as if my last strength has been taken away from me."*

---

[117] Maternus Mallmann to Mauritius Klostermann, Memphis, August 14, 1878, "Letters of Memphis. 1878-1888," Nr. 1a, SHPA.

[118] Ruprecht Honorius to James Meyer, Memphis June 16, 1928, SHPA Lucius Buchholz' personal file.

[119] D. A. Quinn, "Heroes and Heroins: Brave Deeds of Priests and Sisters at Memphis During the Epidemic," in *Catholic News*, 1897, SHPA.

What a contrast to the joyful and positive letters from Friars such as Servatius Altmicks or Heribert Mertens. In his letter, Buchholz calls the American Mission a "leaky boat" that only Janknecht could hold together. Otherwise he predicted a great exodus to Holland. And then he refers to the accusations against himself:

> *"Now something about Memphis. On July 20 I followed the explicit order of the Reverend Bishop and went to Nashville to lead two retreats. I was finished on August 15. About this time, I got news that the Yellow Fever had broken out in Memphis again and that it was raging terribly. Even though I was quite exhausted, I went back immediately. I found the friary in great disorder. Everybody had sombre faces. Nobody spoke a word. On the fifth day I felt the fever coming. I took the right medicine and called for Dr. Willet. He explained that I would be lost if I continued to go out. He urged me to leave the city. That would be my only rescue. He explained that Aloys would be the best man to substitute for me since he had had the Fever already in 1873 and could not get infected a second time. Finally I decided to send a telegraph to the Commissary. He answered that I could leave. He left the decision up to my conscience. And now I leave it up to your conclusion, dear Pater Reverende, to judge, if I have greatly failed. I have been back in Memphis for three months already. P. Aloys and P. Hermann have presented me as a runaway in front of the Friars and the Sisters."[120]*

His letter conveys a totally different impression than the comments about his flight which are quoted above. Buchholz did not run away from danger. When he became infected with the deadly disease, he asked for permission to leave the city. He had already experienced the Yellow Fever epidemic in 1873 and seen the thousands of dead and had buried them. When the Yellow Fever returned in 1879 he stayed in town before he returned to the Mother Province in 1880.[121] For some of the Friars, the challenging life in the American Commissariat meant joyful fulfilment. They were needed and could help. Others, however, did not care for the difficult living conditions in America. They suffered and some of them even broke down or fled.

In November 1878 Janknecht offered the Friars of the North American Commissariat the option of returning to their Mother

---

[120] Lucius Buchholz to Gregory Janknecht, Memphis Dec. 16, 1878, in ASFP Werl.

[121] See Personal file Fr. Lucius Buchholz, in SHPA, Nr. 63.

Province while the Commissariat became an independent Province. Most of the Friars responded to this offer with a brief Yes or No. But some of the Friars took the time to explain their decisions—mostly Friars who wanted to return to Europe. In some cases these are the only written testimonials that remain from these Friars. However, they provide another honest insight into Franciscan life in the American mission. Furthermore, they document what disturbed the Friars, what they struggled with in the New World, and what they missed.

It is not surprising that there were Friars wishing to go back. In general, every major era of immigration was followed by a return movement.[122] The number of Germans who returned from America range from 4.7 percent in 1859 to 49.4 percent in 1875. The average number of returnees was around 6.6 percent in the 1850s, 22.3 percent in the 1870s, and 14.2 percent in the 1880s.[123] But while the majority of German immigrants came to the U.S. for economic reasons, the Saxonian Franciscans had been expelled from their home country because of the *Kulturkampf*. Most of them never regarded their residence in America as the start of a new existence but rather as exile. For some of the Friars the expulsion was a welcome chance to go into the mission. Others came to terms with their lives in America. But most of the Friars never intended to spend the rest of their lives in the U.S. They hoped to return to their original friaries as soon as possible. Fulgentius Hansen's letter makes this quite clear. He was not happy about his immigration and had reluctantly submitted to his fate:

[122] For a long time German immigration to the U.S. was regarded as a one-way street. The return migration was only treated as a peripheral phenomenon. It is only since the 1980s that historians researched the German return migration. Karen Schniedewind, *Begrenzter Aufenthalt im Land der unbegrenzten Möglichkeiten. Bremer Rückwanderung aus Amerika 1850-1914* (Stuttgart, 1994), 9.

[123] Günter Moltmann, "American-German Return Migration in the Nineteenth and Early Twentieth Centuries," in *Central European History* (1980), 383. These numbers however do not differentiate between business travellers and immigrants who returned to their home country. While Moltmann believes this distortion is small, Kamphoefner thinks the numbers are too high. Kamphoefner on the other hand has only regional statistics for Bavaria and Wurttemberg. See Walter D. Kamphoefner, „Umfang und Zusammensetzung der deutsch-amerikanischen Rückwanderung," in *Amerikastudien* (1988), 296-299.

> *"I went to America with an aversion for the country. This has abated during the year, but it has not turned into love for the country and its conditions. After having spent the biggest part of my life in Parish ministry, I believe that a priest can only be effective when he loves the country and its people. Besides that I have always tried not to become attached too close to this country. Furthermore, there are some very gruesome cases in the Province."*[124]

This letter elucidates another Franciscan dilemma: The Friars were not prepared for the demanding work in the parishes, so they longed all the more to get back to their quiet German friaries.

Other friars also wanted to go back to the Mother Province for other reasons. Dominicus Rheidt asked to be sent back to Europe because of his health:

> *"Unfortunately my health has not improved. The tumour on my foot has eased a little over the last weeks. But now I am suffering from rheumatic pains and headaches. My memory is frail so that I can hardly remember the easiest things. Suddenly I feel dizzy and I am in danger of falling. Just recently I had two attacks during Holy Mass. If you regard it as appropriate to send me to Hot Springs, I am willing to go. But let me make another suggestion. A cruise and a complete change of climate might be the best treatment for me. I have often thought about going back to Europe. But I was too timid to ask because I think I am not worth the travel costs anymore. On the other hand I cannot achieve anything here anymore and then you would be rid of one nuisance."*[125]

Several other Franciscans also referred to health problems as reasons for their return to Europe. Some report of vomiting blood. Some complained of the extreme climate. Br. Mauritius Kruse writes:

> *"I only want to mention one of the reasons that would allow me to go back: You, Reverend Father, know from your own experience, that the summers get very hot. This summer we had 104 Fahrenheit in Jordan. We have to work and pray, but both are almost impossible under this heat."*[126]

---

[124] Fulgentius Hansen to Mauritius Klostermann, St. Louis Jan. 1, 1879, in ASFP Werl. Hansen left the Order in 1884.

[125] Dominicus Rheidt to Vincent Halbfaß, Rhineland, July 14, 1880, in SHPA.

[126] Mauritius Kruse to Mauritius Klostermann, Jordan Jan. 1, 1879, in ASFP Werl. Kruse returned to Europe in 1880.

Some of the priests in pastoral care also complained about their lack of effectiveness due to their poor language skills. P. Pancratius Schulte wrote:

"The greatest obstacle to my effectiveness is the English language. I often feel this deficiency, not only in mixed parishes but also in German parishes. In particular, the youth speak less and less German. Even in the confessional they use the English language."[127]

Another motive for return was the yearning for family. Remigius Goette, who came to America in 1875 together with his two brothers, and whose sisters who had fled to France when the *Kulturkampf* started, calls this the love he owed to his parents:

"When my brothers and I left Germany, my parents wished that we would return from America. This desire has not ceased over the years since then. In his last letter our father repeated his wish to see us once again."[128]

Some of the friars decided to stay in America as long as the *Kulturkampf* was still going on and there was little need for them in Holland or Belgium. Augustinus Henseler writes:

"I am writing these lines only for the purpose that you may not get the impression that I am already fully Americanized and would stay forever. If you or your successor can find an occupation for me in Europe, I would be more than content to go back, especially when our Mother Province gets back its friaries someday."[129]

Some of the Friars left the decision up to the General or Provincial Minister. Franziskus Haase wrote:

[127] Pancratius Schulte to Mauritius Klostermann, Indianapolis Jan. 3, 1879, in ASFP Werl. Despite his plea Schulte was not sent back to Germany. He stayed in America and died in Cleveland in 1913.

[128] Remigius Goette to Mauritius Klostermann, St. Louis Jan. 10, 1879, in ASFP Werl. Goette went back to Europe in 1881. From there he went to the mission in China. In 1880 his two brothers had already gone directly from America to China and stayed there throughout their lives. His brother Athanasius Goette became the first American Bishop in China.

[129] Augustinus Henseler to Mauritius Klostermann, Cleveland Dec. 31, 1878, in ASFP Werl.

"The General should take the decision. Some of the Friars have already asked the General or still want to ask him. They should briefly inform the Reverend Definitorium of this Province about this step."[130]

The responses to the offer to return reveal a broad spectrum of attitudes: There are all kinds of motives from tender wishes to see one's family to health problems to open aversion toward the U.S. In a letter to the Minister General, Janknecht reported the number of Friars wishing to return as 32: 16 Priests, nine Clerics and seven Lay Brothers.[131] If this number referred only to the Friars who came to America during the *Kulturkampf*—some of whom were already dead—that would mean a very high percentage of returnees. However, you have to consider the Franciscans who already lived in the U.S. when the refugees of *Kulturkampf* arrived. Some of these early Friars may have expressed the wish to return to their Mother Province when the new Province was founded. Thus, the percentage of returnees is most likely somewhere between 20 and 25 percent. This is close to Moltmann's estimation of 22.3 percent during the 1880s.[132]

Janknecht believed he should allow all Friars who wished to do so to return to the Mother Province for the following reasons: *"1. to staff the friaries which we left in Prussia when we get them back with God's support. 2. that the Mother Province may have at least a few capable Friars besides all the less capable ones."*[133] Nevertheless, Janknecht wanted the Friars to stay in America and work there for the time being. Nobody was to return to Europe without special permission.[134]

However, Janknecht's departure from the office of Provincial in 1879 changed the relationship between the Mother Province and the young American Province as well as on the return of the Friars. While Janknecht had always been very fond of the American Mission and visited several times, the new Provincial, Othmar Maasmann, had no strong attachment to America. In the summer of 1880 the Saxonian Provincial began to call back the Friars by telegram. Among those recalled was Lucius Buchholz, who was still Guardian in

---

[130] Franziskus Haase to Vincent Halbfaß, St. Louis Dec. 28, 1880, in SHPA.

[131] Janknecht to General, Febr. 6, 1879 in: Reinhold, Korrespondenz, 74; Habig speaks of 26 Friars who wanted to go back, compare: Habig, *Heralds*,171f.

[132] Compare footnote 126.

[133] Janknecht to General, Febr. 6, 1879 in: Reinhold, Korrespondenz, p. 74.

[134] Janknecht to General, Febr. 6, 1879 in: Reinhold, Korrespondenz, p. 74.

Memphis at that time.[135] Obviously, this had not been coordinated with the Superiors of the Sacred Heart Province. Consequently, the Definitoriums of the two Provinces got into intense arguments about the recall of Friars. While the Saxonian Province filled their friaries in Holland and Belgium with returnees from America, the newly established American Province feared losing its best people.

Thus, the American Province informed the Mother Province that the return of Friars could not take place at once, but needed to be more gradual so that they did not lose too much manpower at the same time.[136] Furthermore, the American Provincial leadership cited Janknecht's promise not to call the Friars back before the end of the Prussian *Kulturkampf*. But the new Saxonian Provincial leadership did not consider itself bound by that promise: "*The call-back of Friars belonging to the Mother Province is by no means dependent on the end of the Kulturkampf.*"[137] In addition, several Friars had written individually to the Saxonian Provincial and had asked to be recalled without letting the American Provincial know. One of these Friars was Lucius Buchholz.[138]

In spite of the ongoing quarrel, some of the Friars returned to the Dutch and Belgian friaries. At the end of the *Kulturkampf* the remaining Friars in the American Province were again asked if they wanted to return to Europe. Seven Priests and one Brother decided to go back. All together, 40 Friars returned to Europe. Almost all of the returnees were Friars who had come to America during the course of the *Kulturkampf*. Taking into account those who died and the Friars who had left the Order, there remained in the Sacred Heart Province fewer than half of the Franciscans who had arrived in 1875 and 1876.[139]

---

[135] Definitorium of the Sacred Heart Province to the Definitorium of the Holy Cross Province, St. Louis Dec. 30, 1880, in ASFP Werl.

[136] Definitorium of the Sacred Heart Province to the Definitorium of the Holy Cross Province, St. Louis Sept. 30, 1880, in ASFP Werl.

[137] Definitorium of the Holy Cross Province to the Definitorium of the Sacred Heart Province, Kerkrade Nov. 24, 1880, in SHPA.

[138] Definitorium of the Sacred Heart Province to the Definitorium of the Holy Cross Province, St. Louis Dec. 30, 1880, in ASFP Werl.

[139] The number of returning Franciscans cannot be compared to that of other immigrants. For many refugees of the *Kulturkampf* life in the U.S. was only a stopgap since there was neither space nor occupation for them in the Dutch and Belgian friaries. Consequently, the majority of Franciscans coming to the U.S. always intended to return to Germany after the end of the *Kulturkampf*.

By the end of the 1870s the Prussian *Kulturkampf* had lost its intensity. Bismarck realized that he could not achieve his goals. Socialism was now a bigger threat than the Catholic Church.[140] Pope Leo XIII also eased the tensions with Prussia. After his election in 1878 he signalled his willingness to negotiate. Issues such as the education of Priests and political proceedings still delayed the revocation of the May Laws. That is the reason why it took until 1887 before Catholic Orders and Congregations could accept new members in Prussia. The Franciscans were affected by the second Peace Law of April 29, 1887.[141] This law allowed them to help out in Parishes. Furthermore, they were allowed to accept citizens of the Reich as members of the Order. The government reserved to itself the limitation of the number of residences and demanded an annual census of the members.[142]

Even before the Law was proclaimed on May 30, 1887, Irenäus Bierbaum,[143] as current Provincial Minister, summoned a meeting of the Definitorium. In addition he had informed the Bishops that the Franciscans wished to return to their home dioceses. Starting in June 1887 the Franciscans could move into their former convents again. They were supposed to support the secular priests especially in larger Parishes.[144] Between the end of the *Kulturkampf* and the beginning of the First World War the Franciscans founded 19 new residences.[145]

When the Franciscans returned to Prussia from exile, there was still the question of military service for the younger Friars. Those who had immigrated as minors committed a criminal offense if they did not report for military service in Prussia before they turned 20 years old. Thus when they returned to Prussia their immediate arrest was imminent, however the Franciscans were supported by Bishop

---

[140] Rakemann, Janknecht, 240f.

[141] The first Peace Law had started the revision of the May Laws. The second law was supported by the Centre Party. If it had not been accepted, the Centre Party had not approved the increase of the armed forces for more than three years. Georg Franz, *Kulturkampf. Staat und Katholische Kirche in Mitteleuropa von der Säkularisation bis zum Abschluß des Preußischen Kulturkampfes* (München, 1954), 269-271.

[142] Fleckenstein, Franziskaner, 64.

[143] Originally, Bierbaum had also been in the U.S. But in 1877 he was called back to Europe in order to support the leadership of the Mother Province.

[144] Fleckenstein, Franziskaner, 65f.

[145] Fleckenstein, Franziskaner, 69.

Kopp. Provincial Bierbaum made clear that the young Friars would not return to Germany if they were to be called up for military service. The Defense Department did not want to give a general exemption from military service for members of Catholic Orders. This would have contradicted the military laws of the Reich. In the end the Frairs received a special permission to serve as male nurses. Thus they did not have to use weapons.[146]

The Franciscans were able to resume their lives in the Order as they had before the *Kulturkampf*. The remains of the *Kulturkampf* were the obligatory civil wedding, the supervision of schools by the State, the Jesuits' Law, the law about the finances of Catholic Parishes and the law about leaving the Church. Furthermore, the Government insisted upon its right to be informed about the members of the churches and its right to object to the appointment of Parish Priests.[147]

5.Conclusion

In the light of these developments, Janknecht's previously quoted circular from the time of the expulsion appears remarkably as a consolation. In June 1875 he had written to the Friars in the Saxonian Province: *"We are confident that this persecution will not lead to the expected decline of our Province, but rather to the promotion and spread of the Kingdom of God."*[148]

After twelve years the *Kulturkampf* was over. The Friars could now return to their original friaries. Indeed, the Saxonian Province of the Holy Cross did not come to an end. Instead it had spread despite unfavourable circumstances and had left behind an independent Daughter Province in the United States. The *Kulturkampf* simply afforded the occasion for the migration of more than 120 Franciscans to the U.S. They mainly came to America because the friaries in Holland and Belgium could not host them. But the main reason for their successful mission was the great number of German immigrants

---

[146] Fleckenstein, Franziskaner, 68.

[147] Franz, *Kulturkampf*, 277f.

[148] Janknecht to the General Minister, June 3, 1875 (Reinhold, Julius: Aus der römischen Korrespondenz des P. Gregor Janknecht über die Jahre 1871-1879. In *Vita Seraphica* 29 [1948] 47-82, here 54).

who had settled in the Midwest. Among them was a large number of Catholics who were left alone without German speaking pastors. This provided many ministerial opportunities for the Friars. There was a great need for priests. Consequently, the priests often became responsible for very large parishes and had to travel extensively.

Their responsibilities in the New World also brought about various changes in their lives as Friars. This concerned very ordinary things such as the use of horses and of money. Special dispensations had to be obtained from Rome, otherwise, the Friars would not have been able to travel in the vast country. Thus, the Rule of the Order had to be adapted to the needs of the new situation in America. Even more significant was the change in the nature of their ministry. In Prussia the Franciscans had not served as pastors of individual Parishes but only helped out as needed. In America the missionaries served the German speaking population as their pastors. This contradicted the spirit of the Order because these Priests were no longer subordinate only to their Superior, but also to the Bishop. Nevertheless, the Franciscans accepted the pastorates of various American parishes because of the need that was there.

Furthermore, many European Friars were not used to the demands of missionary work. In Europe they did not have to give several sermons a day or listen to confessions for hours at a time. In America they had to travel long distances and had to live under primitive and dangerous conditions. Some of the Friars found fulfilment in these circumstances. They were happy for the demanding responsibilities which tested their faith. But others could not abide these demands. They yearned for their previous life in the Mother Province. Some of these left the Order while others became sick and even died. Of the Friars who had come to America during the *Kulturkampf*, only half of them were still there when the *Kulturkampf* ended. The majority of immigrant Friars regarded America only as a temporary exile. From the very beginning they had hoped to return to Germany. This explains the difference between the immigration of 1858 and the flight of 1875. In this regard it might be interesting for future research to examine the transfer processes initiated by those Friars who returned to Germany: Which ideals and opinions did they bring back from America to the European Order? Did they easily fit back into the Order in Europe or did they cause problems?

Besides their adaptation to American conditions, the Franciscans also exported their culture. As a missionary scientist, Otto Maas wrote about the North American mission in an article for the *Jahrbuch des Reichsverbandes für die katholischen Auslandsdeutschen 1933/34*:

"The Friars founded churches and friaries and primarily took care of their fellow country-men. They did not only preach in German, but also founded German speaking churches, schools, associations and newspapers. They were always intent on preserving and promoting German-ness."[149]

Father Beda Kleinschmidt—Provincial of the Saxonian Province from 1915 until 1919—wrote about the labours of the Franciscans among the German immigrants in North America:

"All secular and Order Priests born in Westfalia have earned great merits for preserving German-ness in North America through the foundation and maintenance of German Parish schools. At these schools religion and several other secular subjects were taught in German. That is how they practised and learned to love their Mother tongue. It is mainly due to the German priests, that the German language did not go down in certain places."[150]

Consequently, the Franciscans had a great impact on preserving the German language and culture among the German immigrants.

But most of all, the Franciscan exodus had a great impact on their American mission. When the exile Friars arrived in Teutopolis in 1875, the number of Friars in the mission nearly doubled. This posed a major problem to the Superiors: How to host all these Friars in the existing houses? But in the end it enabled the Order to accept new parishes and found new friaries. Between 1875 and 1879 ten new friaries were opened and four other houses were soon to be

---

[149] Otto Maas, „Die norddeutschen Franziskaner im Auslanddeutschtum," in Jahrbuch des Reichsverbandes für die katholischen Auslanddeutschen 1933/34, 291.

[150] Beda Kleinschmidt, „Von der Arbeit unserer ersten Amerikamissionare unter den Auslandsdeutschen," in *Vita Seraphica* 9 (1928), 43-44. Also: Jürgen Werinhard Einhorn, „Beda Kleinschmidt. Zweimaliger Provinzialminister zwischen 1915 und 1919," in: Dieter Berg (Ed.) *Management und Minoritas. Lebensbilder Sächsischer Franziskanerprovinziale vom Mittelalter bis zum 20. Jahrhundert* (Kevelaer, 2003) (Saxonia Franciscana, Beiheft 1) 320-357.

erected as friaries. Such a big group of Friars was also difficult to manage from Europe. Postal service was slow, and the Friars in America had to ask for permission from their European Superiors for almost everything: the appointment of new Guardians, the admission of new members etc. This made their independence more and more necessary. In 1874 there had already been one request for separation from the Mother Province before the refugees of the *Kulturkampf* arrived.[151] The unexpected arrival of these refugees supported the request for establishment as an independent Province. Consequently, the erection of the Sacred Heart Province is also an effect of the *Kulturkampf*.

Despite the Franciscans' work among the German immigrants, the German character of the Sacred Heart Province diminished with the assimilation of the German immigrants and the decreasing number of new immigrants after 1900. Some of the parishes taken over by the refugees of the *Kulturkampf* are still cared for by Franciscans, but the percentage of Germans among the shepherds as well as among the sheep is now quite small.

[151] Janknecht to General Minister December 12, 1875, Reinhold, *Korrespondenz*, 60.